First World War

and Army of Occupation

War Diary

France, Belgium and Germany

3 DIVISION
Divisional Troops
56 Field Company Royal Engineers
16 August 1914 - 31 May 1919

WO95/1403/1

The Naval & Military Press Ltd
www.nmarchive.com
Published in association with The National Archives

Published by

The Naval & Military Press Ltd

Unit 10 Ridgewood Industrial Park,

Uckfield, East Sussex,

TN22 5QE England

Tel: +44 (0) 1825 749494

www.naval-military-press.com

www.nmarchive.com

This diary has been reprinted in facsimile from the original. Any imperfections are inevitably reproduced and the quality may fall short of modern type and cartographic standards.

Contents

Document type	Place/Title	Date From	Date To
Heading	WO95/1403/1		
Heading	3rd Division 56th Fld Coy. R.E. 1914 Aug-1919 May		
Heading	R.E. 56th Field Coy. War Diary Aug-Dec, 1914		
Miscellaneous	3rd Divnl Engineer		
Heading	121/742 War Diary 56th. Field Co. R.E. 3rd Division Vol. I 16.8-4.9.14		
War Diary		16/08/1914	26/08/1914
Diagram etc	Canal Bridge Between Pontoise And Varesives		
Diagram etc	Top Flange Bottom Hange Similar		
Miscellaneous			
War Diary		27/08/1914	04/09/1914
Heading	121/1084 56th Coy. R.E 3rd Division 5-30.9.14 Volume II		
Heading	War Diary of 56th Field Co RE Covering The Period 5th Sept-30th Sept 1914		
War Diary		05/09/1914	13/09/1914
War Diary	Chassemy	14/09/1914	30/09/1914
Miscellaneous	Following Information Received For ? Hd Qrs.		
Miscellaneous	Instructions Divisional Messages From Commander 9th General		
Miscellaneous	7th Brigade		
Miscellaneous	Special Order Of The Day By Field Marshall Sir John French, G.C.B., G.C.V.O., K.C.M.G., Commander-in-Chief, British Army In The Field.		
Miscellaneous	R.E.		
Miscellaneous	3rd Divn		
Miscellaneous	C Form. (Duplicate.) Messages & Signals.		
Miscellaneous	3rd Divn		
Miscellaneous	C Form. (Duplicate.) Messages & Signals.		
Heading	121/1872 56th Coy: RE 3rd Division Vol III 1-31.10.14		
Miscellaneous	C.R.E. 3rd Divn		
War Diary		01/10/1914	16/10/1914
War Diary	Neuve Chapelle	17/10/1914	23/10/1914
War Diary	Richbourg St Vaast	24/10/1914	31/10/1914
Miscellaneous	56th Co. R.E		
Diagram etc	Works 56th Field Coy RE. Vailly Bridge River Aisne		
Miscellaneous	C Form (Duplicate). Messages And Signals.		
Heading	121/2599 3rd Division 56th Field Coy RE Vol IV. 1-30.11.14		
War Diary	Croix De Popringe	01/11/1914	05/11/1914
War Diary	Loore	06/11/1914	06/11/1914
War Diary	Ypres	07/11/1914	24/11/1914
Miscellaneous	Capt Neville ?		
War Diary		25/11/1914	30/11/1914
Miscellaneous	General Corps		
Miscellaneous	Type of Redoubt Belgian Issue Ponit D'App		
Diagram etc	Redoubt 17 Wood E Of Ypres		
Heading	121/3944 3rd Division 56th Field Coy RE Vol V 1-31.12.14		
War Diary	Kemmel	01/12/1914	02/12/1914

War Diary	Mont Noir-Westoutre	03/12/1914	06/12/1914
War Diary	Westoutre	07/12/1914	09/12/1914
War Diary	Kemmel	10/12/1914	11/12/1914
War Diary	Westoutre	12/12/1914	15/12/1914
War Diary	Kemmel	16/12/1914	18/12/1914
War Diary	Westoutre	19/12/1914	24/12/1914
War Diary	Kemmel	24/12/1914	26/12/1914
War Diary	Westoutre	27/12/1914	31/12/1914
Heading	R.E. 56th Field Coy., War Diary, Jan-Dec., 1915		
Heading	121/4655 3rd Division 56th Field Coy: RE Vol VI 1-31.1.15		
Heading	56th Field Co. R.E. January 1915		
War Diary	Westoutre	01/01/1915	03/01/1915
War Diary	Kemmel	04/01/1915	07/01/1915
War Diary	Westoutre	08/01/1915	27/01/1915
War Diary	Kemmel	28/01/1915	31/01/1915
Diagram etc	Incinerator (For An Infantry Brigade)		
Heading	121/4586 3rd Division 56th Field Coy: RE Vol VIII 1-28.2.15		
War Diary	Mont Noir	01/02/1915	04/02/1915
War Diary	Kemmel	05/02/1915	09/02/1915
War Diary	Mont Noir	10/02/1915	12/02/1915
War Diary	Kemmel	13/02/1915	21/02/1915
War Diary	Mont Noir	22/02/1915	25/02/1915
War Diary	Kemmel	26/02/1915	28/02/1915
Heading	121/4939 3rd Division 56th Field Coy RE Vol VIII 1-31.3.15		
War Diary	Kemmel	01/03/1915	03/03/1915
War Diary	Mont Noir	04/03/1915	13/03/1915
War Diary	Kemmel	14/03/1915	17/03/1915
War Diary	Reninghelst	18/03/1915	31/03/1915
Heading	121/5254 3rd Division 56th Field Coy: R E. Vol IX 1-28.4.15		
War Diary		01/04/1915	28/04/1915
Heading	121/5425 3rd Division 56th Field Coy: RE Vol X 1-31.5.15.		
War Diary	Dickebusch	01/05/1915	13/05/1915
War Diary	Zillebeeke.	13/05/1915	14/05/1915
War Diary	Dickebusch	14/05/1915	14/05/1915
War Diary	Zillebeeke	14/05/1915	14/05/1915
War Diary	Dickebusche	15/05/1915	27/05/1915
War Diary	Ypres	27/05/1915	31/05/1915
Heading	121/6357 56th Field Coy RE Vol XI & XII June & July.		
Heading	August May Missing F A 4.7.21		
War Diary	Ypres.	31/05/1915	25/07/1915
War Diary	Dickebusch	25/07/1915	31/07/1915
Heading	3rd Division 121/7599 3rd Division 56th Co. R.E September 1915 Vol XIII		
Miscellaneous	War Diary 56th Field Co. RE September 1915		
Miscellaneous	War Diary-56th Field Co RE September. 1915.		
Heading	121/7779 3rd Division 56th. Co. R.E. Oct. & Nov. Vol XIV		
War Diary	Dickebusch	01/10/1915	30/11/1915
Heading	56th Co. R.E. Dec Vol XV		
War Diary	Dickebusch	01/12/1915	31/12/1915

Heading	3rd Division War Diary 56th Field Coy R.E. January To December 1916		
Heading	3rd Divisional Engineers. 56th Field Company R.E. January 1916.		
War Diary	Dickebusch	01/01/1916	31/01/1916
Heading	3rd Divisional Engineers. 56th Field Company R.E. February 1916.		
War Diary	Dickebusch	01/02/1916	07/02/1916
War Diary	No Rbe Court	08/01/1916	19/01/1916
War Diary	Oude Ramig	22/02/1916	29/02/1916
Heading	3rd Divisional Engineers. 56th Field Company R.E. March 1916.		
War Diary	Ouderdom.	01/03/1916	16/03/1916
War Diary	Dickebusch	17/03/1916	31/03/1916
Heading	3rd Divisional Engineers. 56th Field Company R.E. April 1916.		
Heading	Vol 19 War Diary of 56th Coy R.E. From April 1st To April 30th 1916.		
War Diary	Dickebusch	01/04/1916	06/04/1916
War Diary	Meteren	06/04/1916	12/04/1916
War Diary	La Clitte	13/04/1916	19/04/1916
War Diary	Meteren	19/04/1916	20/04/1916
War Diary	R.E. Farm	20/04/1916	25/04/1916
War Diary	N 15.c.2.3 R E Farm	25/04/1916	30/04/1916
Heading	3rd Divisional Engineers. 56th Field Company R.E. May 1916.		
War Diary	R.E. Farm N.15.c 2.3 (Sheet 28)	01/05/1916	23/05/1916
War Diary	La Clytte N7 C8 10	24/05/1916	31/05/1916
Heading	3rd Divisional Engineers. 56th Field Company R.E. June 1916.		
War Diary	La Clytte N7c8.10 Sheet 10	01/06/1916	20/06/1916
War Diary	Polincove	20/06/1916	01/07/1916
Heading	3rd Divisional Engineers. 56th Field Company R.E. July 1916.		
War Diary	Carnoy	16/07/1916	25/07/1916
War Diary	Sand Pits	26/07/1916	26/07/1916
War Diary	Near Bray	27/07/1916	27/07/1916
War Diary	Ville Sur Ancre	28/07/1916	31/07/1916
War Diary	Polincove	01/07/1916	02/07/1916
War Diary	Rebeaucourt	03/07/1916	03/07/1916
War Diary	Bertangles	04/07/1916	04/07/1916
War Diary	Lahoussie	05/07/1916	05/07/1916
War Diary	Bray	06/07/1916	06/07/1916
War Diary	Carnoy	07/07/1916	15/07/1916
Heading	3rd Divisional Engineers 56th Field Company R.E. August 1916		
War Diary	Ville Sous Corbie	01/08/1916	10/08/1916
War Diary	Sandpits Sheet 57 D (S.E) E 18 d 4.0.	12/08/1916	12/08/1916
War Diary	Sandpits	13/08/1916	13/08/1916
War Diary	Citadel Sheet 57 D (S E) F 15 C 9.3.	14/08/1916	14/08/1916
War Diary	Minden Post Near Carnoy	15/08/1916	19/08/1916
War Diary	Citadel	20/08/1916	20/08/1916
War Diary	Ville Sur Ancre.	21/08/1916	22/08/1916
War Diary	Lanches	23/08/1916	24/08/1916
War Diary	Mezerolles	25/08/1916	25/08/1916
War Diary	Neuville Au Cornet.	26/08/1916	26/08/1916

War Diary	Petit Anvin	27/08/1916	28/08/1916
War Diary	Tangry Marles	29/08/1916	29/08/1916
War Diary	Les Mines	30/08/1916	30/08/1916
War Diary	Mazingarbe	31/08/1916	31/08/1916
Heading	3rd Divisional Engineers. 56th Field Company R.E. September 1916.		
War Diary	Mazingarbe	01/09/1916	20/09/1916
War Diary	Auchel	21/09/1916	22/09/1916
War Diary	Cuhem	23/09/1916	30/09/1916
Heading	3rd Divisional Engineers. 56th Field Company R.E. October 1916.		
War Diary	Cuhem	01/10/1916	04/10/1916
War Diary	Hernicourt	05/10/1916	07/10/1916
War Diary	On Rail	08/10/1916	08/10/1916
War Diary	Beaussart.	09/10/1916	18/10/1916
War Diary	Courcelles	19/10/1916	31/10/1916
Miscellaneous	9th Bde.		
Diagram etc	Wire Third Night		
Diagram etc	Design For "Z" Trench		
Map			
Heading	3rd Divisional Engineers. 56th Field Company R.E. November 1916.		
War Diary	Courcelles	01/11/1916	30/11/1916
Miscellaneous	C R E III Division		
Heading	3rd Divisional Engineers. 56th Field Company R.E. December 1916.		
Miscellaneous	Officer i/c Adjutant General's Office at the Bass.		
Miscellaneous	C R E III Division		
War Diary	Courcelles	01/12/1916	31/12/1916
Heading	3rd Division War Diary 56th F. Coy, January To December 1917		
War Diary	Courcelles	01/01/1917	08/01/1917
War Diary	Beaussart	09/01/1917	27/01/1917
War Diary	Sarton.	28/01/1917	28/01/1917
War Diary	Rebreuve	29/01/1917	31/01/1917
War Diary	Dieval	02/02/1917	28/02/1917
War Diary	Arras	01/03/1917	30/04/1917
War Diary	Tilloy	01/05/1917	14/05/1917
War Diary	Simencourt	15/05/1917	18/05/1917
War Diary	Liencourt	19/05/1917	19/05/1917
War Diary	St Pol	20/05/1917	02/06/1917
War Diary	Camp near Feuchy	03/06/1917	05/06/1917
War Diary	Railway Triangle	06/06/1917	12/06/1917
War Diary	Dugouts N Of Tilloy	13/06/1917	18/06/1917
War Diary	Arras	19/06/1917	20/06/1917
War Diary	Gouyen-Artois	21/06/1917	30/06/1917
War Diary	Achiet-Le-Petit	01/07/1917	02/07/1917
War Diary	Le Bucquiere	03/07/1917	04/09/1917
War Diary	Beaulencourt	05/09/1917	18/09/1917
War Diary	Hopoutre	19/09/1917	19/09/1917
War Diary	Vlamertinghe	20/09/1917	23/09/1917
War Diary	Ypres	24/09/1917	30/09/1917
War Diary	Brandhoek	01/10/1917	01/10/1917
War Diary	Winnezeele	02/10/1917	04/10/1917
War Diary	Wisernes	05/10/1917	05/10/1917
War Diary	Ytres	06/10/1917	08/10/1917

War Diary	Favreuil	09/10/1917	09/10/1917
War Diary	Noreuil	10/10/1917	30/11/1917
War Diary	Favreuil	01/12/1917	11/12/1917
War Diary	Noreuil	12/12/1917	22/12/1917
War Diary	Mory	23/12/1917	31/12/1917
Heading	3rd Division War Diary 56th Field Coy R.Es 1918 Jan-1919 May		
War Diary	Mory	01/01/1918	10/01/1918
War Diary	Henin	11/01/1918	28/01/1918
War Diary	Boiry.	29/01/1918	01/02/1918
War Diary	Becquerelle	01/02/1918	28/02/1918
Heading	3rd Divisional Engineers 56th Field Company R.E. March 1918		
Miscellaneous	C R E 3rd Division	01/04/1918	01/04/1918
War Diary	Boiry Becquerelle	01/03/1918	21/03/1918
War Diary	Wailly	22/03/1918	28/03/1918
War Diary	Grosville	29/03/1918	29/03/1918
War Diary	Gouy-En-artois	30/03/1918	30/03/1918
War Diary	Ivergny	31/03/1918	31/03/1918
Heading	3rd Divisional Engineers War Diary 56th Field Company R.E. April 1918		
War Diary	Ivergny	01/04/1918	01/04/1918
War Diary	Beugin	02/04/1918	04/04/1918
War Diary	Ourton	05/04/1918	07/04/1918
War Diary	Hersin	08/04/1918	11/04/1918
War Diary	Oblinghem	12/04/1918	14/04/1918
War Diary	Annezin	14/04/1918	12/05/1918
War Diary	D.24.a.Central	13/05/1918	16/05/1918
War Diary	Annezin	16/05/1918	30/05/1918
War Diary	D.24.a.Central	31/05/1918	31/05/1918
War Diary			
War Diary	D.24.a.Central	01/06/1918	04/06/1918
War Diary	Annezin	05/06/1918	07/08/1918
War Diary	Raimbert	07/08/1918	13/08/1918
War Diary	Brevillers	14/08/1918	19/08/1918
War Diary	Brevillers Au Bois	20/08/1918	28/08/1918
War Diary	57C. S 10.d.7.4	28/08/1918	05/09/1918
War Diary	St. Leger	06/09/1918	06/09/1918
War Diary	Pommier	07/09/1918	11/09/1918
War Diary	Ablainzeville	12/09/1918	12/09/1918
War Diary	Mort. Homme	13/09/1918	14/09/1918
War Diary	Beugny	16/09/1918	16/09/1918
War Diary	J.26.b.7.6	16/09/1918	30/09/1918
War Diary			
War Diary	Havrincourt	01/10/1918	01/10/1918
War Diary	Flesquieres	09/10/1918	09/10/1918
War Diary	Havrincourt	13/10/1918	13/10/1918
War Diary	Marloing	20/10/1918	20/10/1918
War Diary	Bevillers	22/10/1918	22/10/1918
War Diary	Quievy	23/10/1918	23/10/1918
War Diary	Solesmes	24/10/1918	24/10/1918
War Diary	Romeries	27/10/1918	27/10/1918
War Diary	Escarmain	30/10/1918	30/10/1918
War Diary	Solesmes	31/10/1918	31/10/1918
War Diary	Cattenieres	01/11/1918	03/11/1918
War Diary	Solesmes	04/11/1918	04/11/1918

War Diary	Escarmain	05/11/1918	05/11/1918
War Diary	Orsinval	06/11/1918	16/11/1918
War Diary	La Longueville	18/11/1918	18/11/1918
War Diary	Sous-Le-Bois	20/11/1918	24/11/1918
War Diary	Biercee	25/11/1918	25/11/1918
War Diary	Berzee	26/11/1918	28/11/1918
War Diary	St Gerard	29/11/1918	29/11/1918
War Diary	Durinne	30/11/1918	01/12/1918
War Diary	Durnal	01/12/1918	04/12/1918
War Diary	Scy	05/12/1918	05/12/1918
War Diary	Monteuville	06/12/1918	06/12/1918
War Diary	Fisenne	07/12/1918	07/12/1918
War Diary	Oster-Le-Bally	08/12/1918	08/12/1918
War Diary	Frai Ture	09/12/1918	09/12/1918
War Diary	Hebron val	10/12/1918	11/12/1918
War Diary	Deyfeldt	12/12/1918	12/12/1918
War Diary	Neundorf	13/12/1918	13/12/1918
War Diary	Andler	14/12/1918	14/12/1918
War Diary	Frauenkron	15/12/1918	15/12/1918
War Diary	Blankenheim	16/12/1918	16/12/1918
War Diary	Holzmulheim	17/12/1918	17/12/1918
War Diary	Eversheim	18/12/1918	18/12/1918
War Diary	Kessinich	19/12/1918	19/12/1918
War Diary	Froitzheim	20/12/1918	20/12/1918
War Diary	Duren	21/12/1918	31/12/1918
Miscellaneous	C R E 3rd Division		
War Diary	Duren	01/02/1919	24/02/1919
War Diary	Kerpen	25/02/1919	25/02/1919
War Diary	Cologne	25/02/1919	30/04/1919
Miscellaneous	Confidential	31/05/1919	31/05/1919
War Diary	Cologne	01/05/1919	31/05/1919

3RD DIVISION

56
~~5TH~~ FLD COY. R.E.

~~AUG 1914-DEC 1918~~

1914 AUG – 1919 MAY

Index

SUBJECT.

3RD DIV.

No.	Contents.	Date.
	R. E,	
	56TH FIELD COY.	
	—	
	WAR DIARY	
	AUG - DEC, 1914	

(56,425). Wt.24,741—161. 2000. 11/20. Gp.164. A.&E.W.

Asst. Adjt.
3rd Divnl Engineers

Herewith the War Diary of the Company, completed up to the present date. Owing to the loss of all writing materials the details in some cases have had to be supplied from memory.

J. J. [illegible]
Capt. R.E.
O.C. 56 Co. R.E.

La MOTE FM

5.9.14

75

War Diary

121/742

56th Field Co. R.E. 3rd Division.

Vol. I 16.8 – 4.9.14.

Instructions regarding War Diaries and Intelligence Summaries are contained in F.S. Regs. Part II and the Staff Manual respectively. Title pages will be prepared in manuscript.

WAR DIARY.

~~OR~~

~~INTELLIGENCE SUMMARY.~~

(Erase heading not required.)

Army Form C. 2118. 1

56th Field Company R.E.

Hour, Date, Place.	Summary of Events and Information.	Remarks and References to Appendices
August 16th 1914 (Sunday) –	The Company entrained at Amesbury Station at 8 a.m for Southampton. Arrived Southampton about mid-day & commenced embarking on S.S. FAUVETTE at once. The ship sailed about 6 p.m, reporting at SANDOWN BAY Examination Anchorage before proceeding to sea.	The Officers belonging to the Co. are Maj N.T. Hopkins R.E. (in Command) Capt J.J. Walton " Lieut C.G. Moores " " C.G. Martin " J.A. Leventhorpe " H.W. Holt R.E. S.R.
" 17th –	Arrived ROUEN about 3 p.m, commenced disembarking	
" 18th –	Disembarkation completed. The Coy proceeded to the Champ de Bruyère rest camp, about 3 miles from the Quai	
" 19th –	The Coy entrained 4.30 a.m at Rouen Station & proceeded to LANDRECIES to join the 3rd Divn Expeditionary Force arriving there about 6 p.m, the Coy spent the night partly in billets & partly in bivouac	
" 20th	The Coy proceeded by march route with the Division to DOMPIERRE	Length of march 13 M
" 21st	ditto ditto GROGNIES	" " 18 M
" 22nd	ditto ditto MESVIN	" " 8 M
	During the latter march No1 Sectn under Lieut Moores was attached to 8th Bde & spent the night at VILLIERS GUESLIN, some entrenchments & wire entanglement were constructed during the night. No2 Sectn (Lt Leventhorpe) was attached to 2d Middlesex & spent the night at BETTIGNIES, subsequently moving forward with the Adv Guard	

Instructions regarding War Diaries and Intelligence Summaries are contained in F.S. Regs Part II and the Staff Manual respectively. Title pages will be prepared in manuscript.

WAR DIARY.
OR
~~INTELLIGENCE~~ SUMMARY.
(Erase heading not required.)

Army Form C. 2118.

Hour, Date, Place.	Summary of Events and Information.	Remarks and References to Appendices
	No 3 Sectn under Lt Martin spent the day working on defences at GIVRY with 8th Inf. Bde. afterwards returning to Coy Hd Qrs at MESVIN. No 4 Sectn accompanied No 2 Sectn	
Aug. 23 (Sunday)	Battle of Mons. Nos 1, 3 & 4 Sectns were ordered to prepare bridges over the canal from NIMY Eastwards for demolition, the work however was not to be carried out without the direct order of a Staff Officer 3rd Divn. None of the sections succeeded owing to finding the enemy in force at all the bridges. At the end of the day the Coy retired to Bivouac at NOUVELLES with the 8th Inf Bde & prepared a position for defence there during the night.	The casualties on this day were Lt Holt & 21 N.C.O's & men missing & 1 limbered wagon. Lt Holt said to be wounded
24.	The enemy attacked NOUVELLES with gun fire at dawn, About 10 o'c the order for retirement was given when the Coy proceeded with the 8th Bde to St WAAST, BAVAY. The Hd Qrs British Expeditionary Force was at BAVAY on this day	March 15 M.
25th	The Coy proceeded by march route to CAUDRY arriving about 8.30 p.m	March about 20 m.
26th	Battle of CAUDRY. The Coy assisted in preparing the	

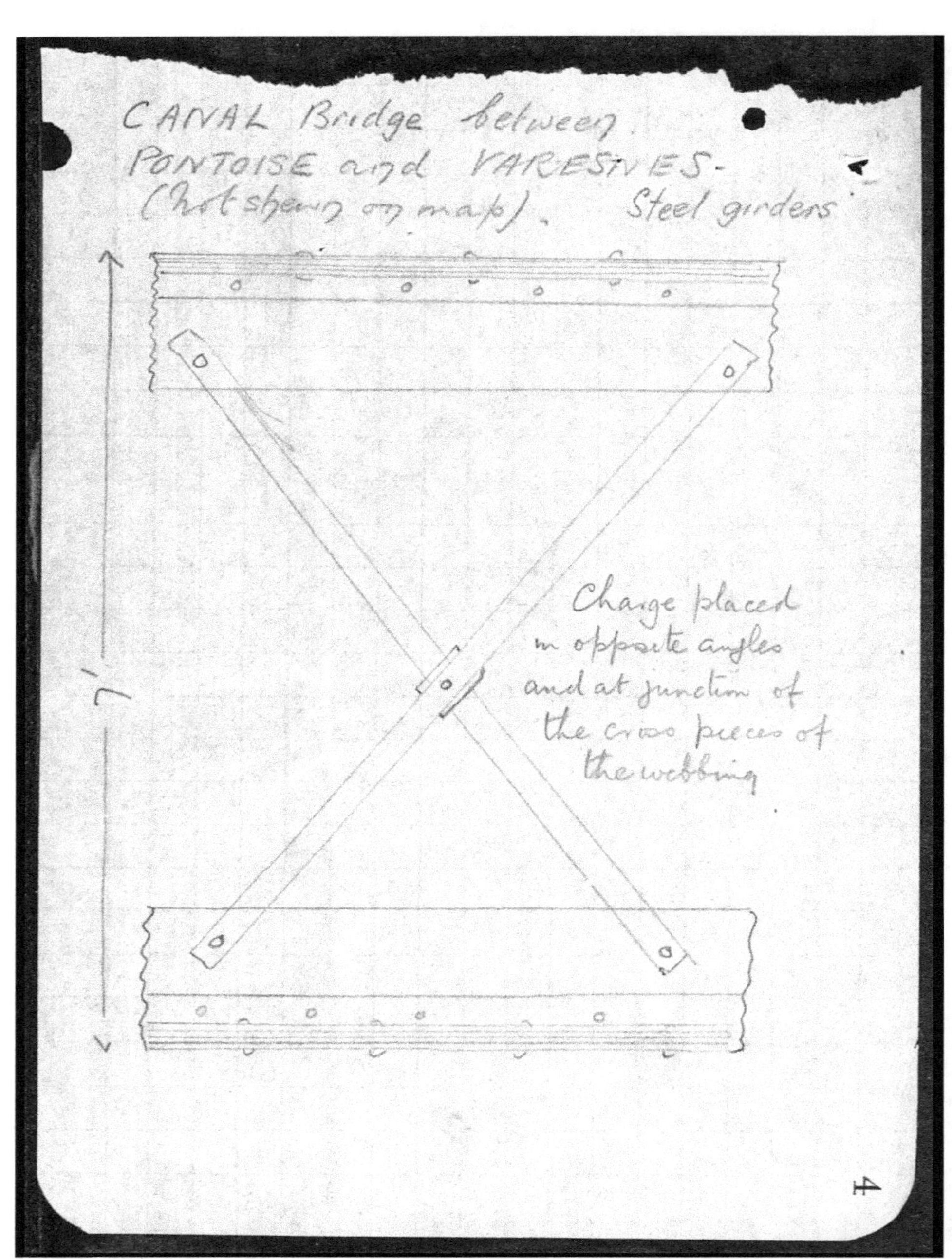
CANAL Bridge between
PONTOISE and VARESNES-
(not shewn on map).
Steel girders
7'
Charge placed in opposite angles and at junction of the cross pieces of the webbing
4

No. Date Time Place

TO Top flange Place

Bottom flange similar

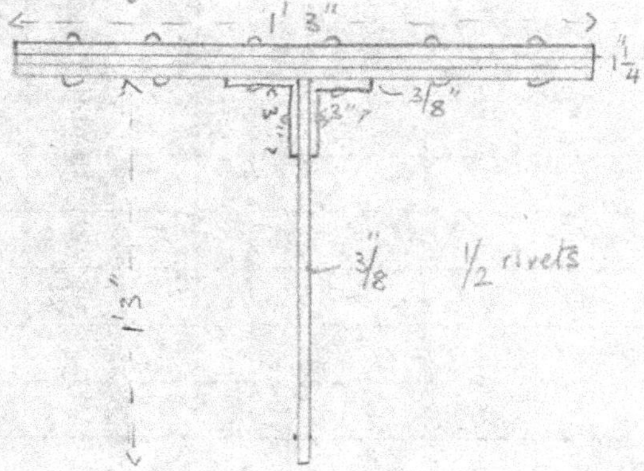

Flanges connected by X webbing ½ plate

Roadway about 15' wide
Wheeltracks supported by longitudinal girders I believe 1' deep 4" flange
No charge placed on these girders
The destruction was complete

From

$3/2\ Bl^{-2}$

Top flange

$$= 3/2 \times \frac{57}{96} \times \left(2\tfrac{1}{8}\right)^2 + 3/2 \times \frac{63}{96} \times \left(1\tfrac{3}{4}\right)^2$$

$$= 3/2 \left(\frac{57 \times (17)^2}{96 \times 64} + \frac{63 \times 49}{96 \times 16} \right)$$

$$= 3/2 \left(5 \text{ lbs} \right) = \frac{15}{2} = 7\tfrac{1}{2} \text{ lbs}$$

Vertical of flange

$$= 3/2 \times 1 \times (3/8)^2 + 3/2 \times \tfrac{1}{4} \times \left(\tfrac{9}{8}\right)^2$$

$$= 3/2 \times \frac{9}{64} + 3/2 \times \frac{1}{4} \times \frac{81}{64}$$

$$\doteq 1 \text{ lb say}$$

$8\tfrac{1}{2}$ lbs + 50% = 12 lbs

Charge used each girder

Top flange	12 lbs
Centre webbing	6 lbs
Bottom flange	12 lbs

Total 60 lbs

33

Instructions regarding War Diaries and Intelligence Summaries are contained in F.S. Regs Part II and the Staff Manual respectively. Title pages will be prepared in manuscript.

WAR DIARY
OR
INTELLIGENCE SUMMARY.
(Erase heading not required.)

Army Form C. 2118.

Hour, Date, Place.	Summary of Events and Information.	Remarks and References to Appendices
	outer buildings of the village for defence & subsequently took its place in the firing line with the Infantry.	Casualties at this battle included Maj Hopkins & Lt Leventhorpe wounded, 8 men missing, believed to be wounded.
	Capt Nation was detailed to take charge of a section of the 57th Co R.E & assist in preparing the defences of the position at AUDENCOURT	During the retirement, the Technical Wagon, 1 limbered wagon, 1 supply wagon & 1 cook's wagon were abandoned by order of a Staff Officer.
	At dusk, the retirement was ordered to BEAUREVOIR where the Coy arrived about 11 p.m. 13 miles	
Augst 27th	At 12.30 a.m. a further retirement was ordered to ~~[illegible]~~ MUILLE about 21 M. which was reached about 7 p.m.	Capt Nation assumed Command of the Coy
" 28th	The Coy marched to PONTOISE	March 14 m.
" 29th	The Coy rested till 4 p.m. after which it proceeded to CUTS to join the 7th Bde. Lt Moores spent the night at VARESNES & prepared the bridge there for demolition with the assistance of some men of the 59th Co R.E. This Bridge was destroyed in the early morning of 30th inst	Details of Bridge attached
" 30th (Sunday)	The Coy was attached to the 8th Inf Bde & marched with it to COURTIEUX	March 16 M.
" 31st	Marched with 8th Inf. Bde to VAUMOISE	" 15 M
Sept 1st	ditto ditto CHEVREVILLE	" 14 M
2nd	ditto 7th Inf Bde MONTHYON	" 9 M.

Instructions regarding War Diaries and Intelligence Summaries are contained in F.S. Regs Part II and the Staff Manual respectively. Title pages will be prepared in manuscript.

WAR DIARY or INTELLIGENCE SUMMARY.

(Erase heading not required.)

Army Form C. 2118.

4

Hour, Date, Place.	Summary of Events and Information.	Remarks and References to Appendices
Sep: 3rd	Marched with 7th Bde as Rear Guard to SANCY. Successive positions prepared to cover the retreat of the 3rd Divn over the R MARNE at MEAUX but these were not attacked by the enemy –	350 lbs guncotton handed over to C.R.E. to demolish bridges at MEAUX. Length of march 12 M:
Sep: 4	The Coy marched again at 10.30 p.m arriving at La Motte FARM at 8 a.m. Sep 4th	Length of march 13 M. The Total strength of the Coy today is 4 Officers 162 other ranks, the following wagons are still deficient 2 limbered wagons, 1 Supply ", 1 Cooks ", 1 Technical ". Two country carts have been requisitioned for temporary use in Carting tools &c. 542 lbs ~~of~~ of guncotton received today to make up deficiencies

AG 7

120/1084

56th Coy: RE

3rd Division

Volume II 5—30.9.14

No suggestions as to equipment

nothing for M.T. ?

War Diary of 56th Field Co R.E

Covering the period

5th Sept – 30th Sept 1914

J.J.H. Nation

Capt RE

O.C. 56th Co R.E.

1.10.14

~~1.10.14~~

Owing to scarcity of stationary it has not been possible to keep a copy of this diary

JN.

Instructions regarding War Diaries and Intelligence Summaries are contained in F.S. Regs. Part II. and the Staff Manual respectively. Title pages will be prepared in manuscript.

WAR DIARY. OR INTELLIGENCE SUMMARY.

(Erase heading not required.)

Army Form C. 2118.

5

Hour, Date, Place.	Summary of Events and Information.	Remarks and References to Appendices
Sept 5	La Motte Farm. The Coy received 2 G.S. wagons & about 570lbs gun cotton to replace deficiencies	
6 Sunday	After 14 days continual retirement, the 3rd Divn received orders to advance. The Coy sent No 1 Sect. with the advanced guard of the 7th Inf Bde. the remainder of the Coy following with the main body. 2 Corps of the enemy are reported in the vicinity, & it is proposed to attack them in conjunction with French troops from the E & W. The Coy camped at FERMOUTIER for the night after a slight brush with the enemy	The attached information was received during the day
7	1 Section detailed to remain with the outposts. 8 cyclists sent along road of advance to clear away barricades erected by the enemy. In the afternoon No 3 Section under Lt Martin was sent off to join the composite Field Co to be commanded by Capt Henderson for the 8th Inf Brigade. At 6 p.m the advance of the 7th Bde was continued to LES PTES AULNOIS 8M	The Strength of the 56th Co R.E. is Now Capt Walton, Lt Moores, Lt Leventhorpe, 119 N.C.O's & men
8	Action at ORLY. The Coy remained with the 7 Bde which was in reserve. About 100 Prisoners were taken by the 3rd Divn today the march was continued to BUSSIERES about 15 M.	The Pontoons of the 56th & 57th Coys arrived in camp tonight – A tobacco ration was issued for the first time today –

Instructions regarding War Diaries and Intelligence Summaries are contained in F.S. Regs Part II and the Staff Manual respectively. Title pages will be prepared in manuscript.

WAR DIARY. OR INTELLIGENCE SUMMARY.

(Erase heading not required.)

Army Form C. 2118. 68

Hour, Date, Place.	Summary of Events and Information.	Remarks and References to Appendices
Sept 9th	The Coy marched at the head of the 7th Bde today, as it was thought that the Bridge over the MARNE might be destroyed by the Germans in their retirement. However this was not the case & the 3rd Divn successfully crossed over at NANTEUIL pressing the enemy back. The Coy went into Bivouacs at BEZU for the night. The 3rd Divn captured 4 German guns today. The 5th Divn unfortunately fired on our troops by mistake taking them for Germans whilst capturing the guns.	The Pontoons were returned to the Divisional Train tonight. Length of march about 10 M. A wet night
10th	The advance was continued today to MONTEFROY, the 9th Bde being in the advance guard & the Coy with the 7th Bde following. 600 prisoners 6 field guns & several maxims fell into the hands of the 3rd Divn.	Length of march about 15 M.
11th	No 2 Sectn was detailed to march with the rear Guard of the 7th Bde to GRAND ROZOY	Lt C F Nation RE joined the Coy today. Length of march 15 M
12th	The Advance was continued to CERSEUIL, arriving in pouring rain. A miserable night	Length of march about 12 M
13th Sunday	The advance was continued towards VAILLY passing through BRAINE. Considerable opposition was met with along the valley of the AISNE as the Germans had taken up a strong	

Army Form C. 2118. 78

Instructions regarding War Diaries and Intelligence Summaries are contained in F.S. Regs Part II and the Staff Manual respectively. Title pages will be prepared in manuscript.

WAR DIARY OR INTELLIGENCE SUMMARY.

(Erase heading not required.)

Hour, Date, Place.	Summary of Events and Information.	Remarks and References to Appendices
	position on the N side. During the night of 13/14 the 56th 57th & Comps Coy R E constructed a pontoon bridge across the river at VAILLY.	
14th CHASSEMY	A Brig of Artillery, Brig of Cav & other troops crossed the bridge at dawn. The 56th Co also crossed & remained for the day in VAILLY which was heavily shelled all the time. In the evening the Coy withdrew to the S. side under fire & camped for the night at CHASSEMY CHATEAU	56 Co R.E had 3 wounded & the interpreter killed
15th	The battle which commenced on the 13th was continued all day. The Coy commenced making fascines for making a heavy pontoon bridge to take mechanical transport. At night the fascines were taken down to the site which was periodically bombarded by the enemy.	A party of 1 N.C.O & 6 men detailed each night to keep the pontoon bridge in order & regulate the traffic
16th	Battle still continued. Fascine making proceeded with & carried down at night as before. No 1 Section was employed at night cutting a path through a wood to enable the Middlesex Regt to take up a position covering the bridge at CONDÉ	

Army Form C. 2118.

WAR DIARY
or
INTELLIGENCE SUMMARY.
(Erase heading not required.)

Instructions regarding War Diaries and Intelligence Summaries are contained in F. S. Regs., Part II. and the Staff Manual respectively. Title pages will be prepared in manuscript.

Hour, Date, Place	Summary of Events and Information	Remarks and references to Appendices
Sep^t 17th	Battle continued all day. Fascine making proceeded with. During the night Lt Leventhorpe & a small party improved the path bridge at VAILLY sufficiently to bring stretchers with wounded across from the N. Side. Lt Watson & a party also improved the plank bridge at the Railway bridge between VAILLY & PRESLES.	18 remounts received to replace casualties among pontoon horses. A few shirts socks & boots also received
18th	Battle continued. Company making fascines all day. At night the fascines were carted down to the site of the proposed new pontoon bridge for mechanical transport	More shirts, socks, boots & tools received for the Coy
19th CHASSEMY	Battle continued. Company making fascines assisted by a working party of 1 Coy Middlesex Reg^t. One of the pontoons of the existing bridge had to be bailed out & a hole made by a shrapnel bullet plugged. This is the first repair the bridge required since construction.	Reinforcement of 1 N.C.O & 20 men received today. The strength of the Coy is now 154 all ranks 68 horses.
20th (Sunday)	The enemy is still holding on to their position on the N side of the AISNE. Fascine making continued by day. At night Lt Watson & Leventhorpe & 30 men were employed at the pontoon bridge regulating & assisting in passing over a continual stream of traffic. 1 N.C.O & 10 men were also employed in making wire entanglements for the Norfolk Reg^t opposite the CONDÉ bridge	

(9 26 6) W 257—976 100,000 4/12 H W V 79/3298

Instructions regarding War Diaries and Intelligence Summaries are contained in F. S. Regs., Part II. and the Staff Manual respectively. Title pages will be prepared in manuscript.

WAR DIARY
or
INTELLIGENCE SUMMARY.
(Erase heading not required.)

Army Form C. 2118.

Hour, Date, Place	Summary of Events and Information	Remarks and references to Appendices
21st	Enemy still on N Side keeping up an intermittent fire. Tried to work small parties on the new bridge site, but the enemy commenced to fire on them & the work had to be suspended. Fascine making proceeded with. Night work on the bridge as before	
22nd	Enemy still holding N Side. 1 N.C.O & 4 men working on approaches to proposed heavy pontoon bridge, remainder of Coy on fascines. At Night Lts Moores & Leventhorpe worked with their Sections on bridge site from 7–10 and 12–4 a.m. The progress of the work was much hampered by a continuous stream of traffic	
23rd	Enemy holding N. Side as above. 1 Offr 1 N.C.O & 12 employed continuously without interruption by the enemy on the Road approaches to the proposed new heavy pontoon bridge for mechanical transport. Remainder of Coy employed making fascines, total number completed to date 450. At Night from 7–10.30 p.m. 2 Sections of the Coy were employed on the approaches on the N bank. Brig. Genl Sandbach visited the work. CHASSEMY	4 men of the Company were wounded by shell fire in camp this evening
24th	Enemy as above. 1 Offr & N.C.O & 12 men employed throughout the day on the approaches to proposed heavy pontoon bridge. From 7 p.m to 10 p.m two sections of the Coy under Lts Moores & Leventhorpe continued the work. At about midnight an ammunition wagon with 4 horse team, went over the side of our original pontoon bridge, damaging 3 bays of superstructure & sinking 1 pontoon. 3 Horses were drowned.	
25th	Enemy as above. 1 Pontoon & 2 bays of superstructure belonging to 12th Co R.E arrived at Bridge site at 4.30 a.m. One section under Lt Walton commenced the work of repair at once. At 5.30 a.m the enemy shelled the	

Instructions regarding War Diaries and Intelligence Summaries are contained in F. S. Regs., Part II. and the Staff Manual respectively. Title pages will be prepared in manuscript.

WAR DIARY
or
INTELLIGENCE SUMMARY.
(Erase heading not required.)

Army Form C. 21[illegible]

Hour, Date, Place	Summary of Events and Information	Remarks and references to Appendices
	bridge a working party, the restoration was however sufficiently carried out by 6 a m to enable light carts & horsemen to pass over the bridge. No work at the bridge was possible during the remainder of the day owing to the enemy's shell fire. From 6.30 p m to midnight Lt Moores & 20 men completed the remainder of the work on the pontoon bridge & improved the ~~remainder~~ road approaches. During this period 4 Battalions passed over the bridge in addition to the nightly supplies, Ammunition, sick & wounded. From midnight to 4.30 a m, the remainder of the Coy assisted by 1 off & 20 men from the Compo. Coy worked on the fascine road approaches for the new heavy bridge.	Sappers Keane & Bunyard & Pioneer Bloomfield brought to notice of C.R.E. for good work on the bridge under fire. See enclosures A, B, C, D
CHASSEMY 26th	Enemy as before. Fascine making continued by day. By night the foot-bridge which had been broken by the heavy traffic of the previous night was repaired. The approaches to the existing pontoon bridge was also improved	
27th (Sunday)	Enemy as before. Fascine making completed (Total number made 450) At mid-day our camp was shelled by the enemy & 1 driver was killed. The men were temporarily removed to a new site but at 5.30 the camp was heavily shelled again 3 horses being killed. The camp was therefore removed to a site near CHASSEMY for the night, the horses being sent to the [illegible] Coy	1 Driver & 3 Horses Killed in Camp
28th	Enemy as before, The company camp was transferred to a new site ½ mile S.E of CHASSEMY, the horses & carts remaining with the [illegible] Coy R.E. 1 mile back on the BRAINE Road. At night the whole company worked on the fascine approaches to the heavy pontoon bridge from 8 p.m to midnight	

Instructions regarding War Diaries and Intelligence Summaries are contained in F. S. Regs., Part II. and the Staff Manual respectively. Title pages will be prepared in manuscript.

Army Form C. 2118.

WAR DIARY
or
INTELLIGENCE SUMMARY.
(*Erase heading not required.*)

Hour, Date, Place	Summary of Events and Information	Remarks and references to Appendices
29th	Enemy as before. Making fascines, pickets & landraids all morning at night 6.30 to 11 p.m. laying road metal on ramp to new heavy pontoon bridge, laying fascines &c. 5 civilian carts requisitioned from Chassemy for use as tip carts. Our camp was shelled again about 6 p.m but no one hurt, it is thought the enemy were searching for a battery ahead & on our flank	There has been considerable difficulty of late in concealing the whereabouts of our camp from the knowledge of the enemy in spite of stringent regulations as to camp fires, lights, concealing horses & vehicles &c. Whether it is spies or clever aeroplane reconnaissance it is difficult to say.
30th CHASSEMY	Enemy as before. The Coy was occupied during the morning, collecting material &c for night work. From 6 p.m to 10 p.m work was continued on the approaches to the proposed heavy pontoon bridge. All fascines practically laid & the ramp down from the canal bridge was covered with road metal, 4 civilian carts being employed for the purpose.	The weather is turning colder especially at night, but possibly owing to plenty of night work & a good supply of provisions, the health of the Coy. is excellent.
		Present strength of Coy 4 Officers 142 N.C.O's & Men 53 Horses
		The total No of Casualties up to date is 52

Following information received from Genl H^d Q^rs

Staff Officer from French 6th Corps has just come in, he reports 2 columns of Germans estimated at 2 Corps marching N. heads of Columns approaching TRILPORT & CHANGIS, the extreme right of 6th French Army is beginning to cross at MEAUX, the remainder of Army is trying to swing round to the E. in order to completely block retirement of Germans over the TRILPORT & CHANGIS Bridges. Those troops who were fighting with 6th French Army last night & this morning have retired in an Easterly direction in disorder.

Received 6.9.14

80

Intercepted wireless message from commander 9th German Corps says his horses are stone cold & his guns worn out with much shooting

Received 6.9.14

7th Brigade · X 3

The Divisional Engineers will in future be organized as 3 companies and a bridging train – The third company will be known as the COMPOSITE Field Co. and will be formed by taking one section from each of the 56th & 57th Cos under the command of Captain HENDERSON – R.E.

The bridging wagons of the 56th & 57th Cos will be brigaded under an N.C.O. and attached to the Divisional Train –

The 3 field Companies will be affiliated to Infantry Brigades, in the same manner as Brigades of Field Artillery as follows.

56th F.C. Co to 7th Infantry Brigade.
Composite F.C. Co to 8th do do.
57th F.C. Co to 9th do do.

This organization will take place from today, the necessary moves being arranged for as soon as possible. 1 section 56th F.C. Co from 7th Brigade area to join 8th Brigade and Capt HENDERSON and one section 57th Co from 9th Brigade area to join 8th Brigade

7th Sept. 1914.

[signature] R.E.
O.C.R.E
III Division –

SPECIAL ORDER OF THE DAY

By FIELD-MARSHAL SIR JOHN FRENCH, G.C.B., G.C.V.O., K.C.M.G.,

Commander-in-Chief, British Army in the Field.

17th September, 1914.

Once more I have to express my deep appreciation of the splendid behaviour of Officers, Non-commissioned Officers and Men of the Army under my Command throughout the great Battle of the Aisne which has been in progress since the evening of the 12th instant. The Battle of the Marne, which lasted from the morning of the 6th to the evening of the 10th, had hardly ended in the precipitate flight of the enemy when we were brought face to face with a position of extraordinary strength, carefully entrenched and prepared for defence by an Army and a Staff which are thorough adepts in such work.

Throughout the 13th and 14th that position was most gallantly attacked by the British Forces, and the passage of the Aisne effected. This is the third day the troops have been gallantly holding the position they have gained against the most desperate counter attacks and a hail of heavy artillery.

I am unable to find adequate words in which to express the admiration I feel for their magnificent conduct.

The French Armies on our right and left are making good progress, and I feel sure that we have only to hold on with tenacity to the ground we have won for a very short time longer, when the Allies will be again in full pursuit of a beaten enemy.

The self-sacrificing devotion and splendid spirit of the British Army in France will [ca]rry all before it.

(Sd.) J. D. P. FRENCH, Field Marshal,

Commanding-in-Chief, The British Army in the Field.

Printing Co., R.E., 39.

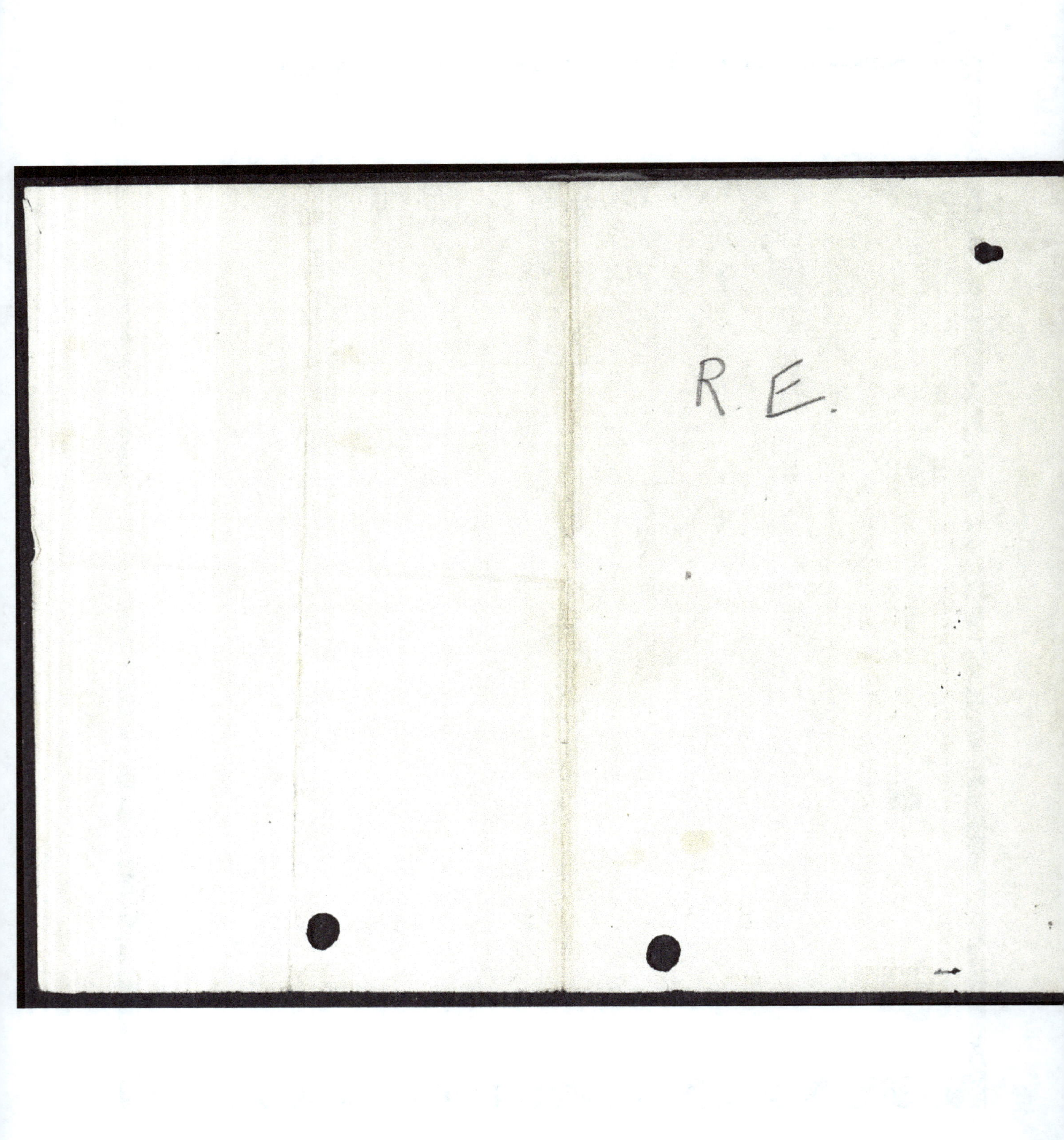
R.E.

(A)

No. Sh MB 63 Date Time Place 12/45am

TO Place O.C. J.S.

3rd Div

VAILLY pontoon Bridge is broken through accident to a wagon. Three bays total forty five feet require repair. Some stores are saved but we still require one pontoon 2 bays of superstructure complete and one chess.

Am applying to Field Co at Chassemy for material and assistance but do not yet know if they can supply

From 8th Bde

25 Sept 12.15AM

From J Buckle Maj BM

C

(5825) Wt. W 7504-1562. 15,000 Pads. Wy. & S., Ltd. Sch. 19. Army Form C 2123.

(B)

C Form. (Duplicate.) **MESSAGES & SIGNALS.** No. of Message ....

Office Stamp.

Inquiries respecting this Message, or application for repetition of the same, may be made at the Delivering Office; but any complaint as to its delay, &c., should be made in writing and addressed to the officer in charge. In either case this form must accompany such inquiries or complaint.

Service Instructions.

Charges to pay £ s. d.

Handed in at the G.T.C *Office at* .M. *Received here at* 1/0 .M.

TO Capt Foster CHASSEMY LODGE

Sender's Number	*Day of Month*	*In reply to Number*	**A. A. A.**
B 815	25		

VAILLY	Ponton	bridge	is	broken
and	one	portion	two	bays
of	[illegible]	[illegible]	are	required
9th	[illegible]	Eng	Co	at
CHASSEMY	has	this	material	do
all	you	can	to	get
it	down	to	the	river
quickly	&	not	let	me
know	[illegible]			

FROM 2nd Div [illegible]

PLACE

TIME

C Copy

3rd Div.n

No material available for repair of pontoon bridge. If 1 pontoon & 2 bays of superstructure can be delivered at the bridge site before daylight I can arrange for repair of bridge

O.C. 56 Co R.E

2.15 a.m.

(5825) Wt. W 7504-1562. 15,000 Pads. Wy. & S., Ltd. Sch. 19.

(D)

Army Form C 2123.

C Form. (Duplicate.)

MESSAGES & SIGNALS.

No. of Message

Mr FRS 13

Office Stamp.

Inquiries respecting this Message, or application for repetition of the same, may be made at the Delivering Office; but any complaint as to its delay, &c., should be made in writing and addressed to the officer in charge. In either case this form must accompany such inquiries or complaint.

25/9/14

Service Instructions.

Charges to pay £ s. d.

Handed in at the QTC *Office at* 6.2 .M. *Received here at* 6.15 .M.

TO 56 Co. R.E.

Sender's Number	*Day of Month*	*In reply to Number*	**A. A. A.**
GA820	25		

Well done

FROM 3rd Div

PLACE

TIME 6.10am

121/1812

56th Coy: RE.

3rd Division

Vol III 1-31.10.14

No. Date Time Place
TO Place

C.R.E.
3rd Divn.

Herewith War Diary of 56th Co R.E. for the month of October.

J. J. Heathcote
Capt R.E.
O.C. 56 Co R.E.

3.11.14.

From

A.G.
Forwarded
3-11-14

G. J. Wills
Capt
Adjt 3rd Div Engrs
for C.R.E.

8

Army Form C. 2118.

Instructions regarding War Diaries and Intelligence Summaries are contained in F. S. Regs., Part II. and the Staff Manual respectively. Title pages will be prepared in manuscript.

WAR DIARY 56th Co R.E.
or
INTELLIGENCE SUMMARY.
(Erase heading not required.)

Hour, Date, Place	Summary of Events and Information	Remarks and references to Appendices
October 1st	Preparing material in the morning for night work on the Bridge. In the afternoon orders were received that the 3rd Divn was going into General Reserve & that the 56 Co R.E was to march with the Worcester Regt from CHASSEMY & rejoin the 7th Inf Bde. This move was however not carried out as the Worcester Regt were unable to hand over their position & get on the move before tomorrow night. The Coy therefore joined the wagons & horses on the BRAINE - CHASSEMY Road & bivouaced there for the night.	Enclosure "Z" gives a general plan of the works on the AISNE when we left them & handed them over to our 1st Army Corps.
2nd	The Coy marched at 6 p.m to SERVENAY picking up 4 pontoons & 4 trestles from the 7th Bridging Coy at BRAINE on the way. The latter are to take over the pontoons that were left in the bridge at VAILLY.	Length of march about 12 M.
3rd	The Coy marched independently at 2 p.m from SERVENAY to CROYOLLES arriving at the latter place at 4 a.m. 25 Miles in 14 hours. A good performance especially considering the bad condition of the roads.	Length of march 25 M.
4th (Sunday)	The Coy marched at 6 p.m to SAINTINES & rejoined 7th Inf Brigade. There was a good deal of difficulty in getting the pontoon wagons along, one of the horses dying on the road from exhaustion	Length of march about 18 M
5th	The Coy entrained after dark each section separately. Two sections at LONGUEIL St MARIE & one section at PONT St MAXENCE at various hours of the night. No information was given as to the destination	

(9 26 6) W 257—976 100,000 4/12 H W V 79/3298

Instructions regarding War Diaries and Intelligence Summaries are contained in F. S. Regs., Part II. and the Staff Manual respectively. Title pages will be prepared in manuscript.

WAR DIARY
or
INTELLIGENCE SUMMARY.
(Erase heading not required.)

Army Form C. 2118.

Hour, Date, Place	Summary of Events and Information	Remarks and references to Appendices
6th	The Coy remained in the train all day & spent the night at the halt in a siding	
7th	The Coy detrained at different stations in the neighbourhood of ABBEVILLE and proceeded to OUVILLE to join 7th Bde. Divisional Hd Qrs are at ABBEVILLE	6? draught horses recd
8th	Received orders to be prepared to march at night **Second Phase of Campaign**	L.Corpl Winton of the Coy received his commission as 2nd Lieut in the Suffolk Regt.
9th	The Coy marched with the 7th Inf Brigade at 1.16 a.m to RENAUGVILLE arriving there about 6 a.m. The mounted portion marched off again at 5.30 p.m with all the mounted troops of the Brigade for PRESSY LES PERNES. #	Distance about 12 M. The Pontoons have joined the Divisional Amm. Column & are to march with them.
10th	The mounted portion of the Coy arrived at PRESSY LES PERNES at 6 a.m making a total march of about 35 miles in 24 hours. The dismounted portion of the Coy were brought direct from RENAUGVILLE in motor lorries arriving at PERNES about 10 a.m.	Medium draught horses are useless for pontoons, they must have the heaviest draught horses & there should never be less than six horse teams
11th (Sunday)	The Coy marched off at 9.40 a.m with the main body of the 3rd Div. to HINGES. No enemy were met with although it was expected that they might make a stand on the LYS Canal.	

Instructions regarding War Diaries and Intelligence Summaries are contained in F. S. Regs., Part II. and the Staff Manual respectively. Title pages will be prepared in manuscript.

WAR DIARY
or
INTELLIGENCE SUMMARY.
(Erase heading not required.)

Army Form C. 2118.

5th Fd. Coy.

Hour, Date, Place	Summary of Events and Information	Remarks and references to Appendices
12th	The Company marched with the right column which consisted of the 7th Bde. One Section being with the advanced guard. Some resistance was met with at LACOUTURE where we relieved the French Cavalry, no further advance was possible tonight. The 8th & 9th Brigades are on our left at LA VIEILLE CHAPELLE & the 5th Div on our right.	
13th	The position remains much the same as yesterday, only very slight advance being made by the Infantry. From prisoners taken we have ascertained that a Jäger Battalion & the Death Head Hussars & a battery of Artillery are in front of us.	Self & Sgt Tankerville rec^d Legion of Honour.
14th	The general position remains the same. In the evening it was decided that the Infantry should push forward from their position at dawn. A number of light plank bridges were made by the Company out of ladders & planking & these were taken out to the Infantry firing line under cover of darkness for use in crossing dykes &c.	Maj Genl Hubert Hamilton C B Commanding our Division was killed by a shrapnel bullet whilst visiting the advanced Infantry line. The Coy made the coffin & he was buried in LACOUTURE Cemetery.
15th	Only a slight advance was possible today, owing to the enemy sticking to the houses in front from which they continually sniped our men. In the evening our gunners shelled the houses.	
16th	It was found this morning that the enemy had evacuated the houses they occupied yesterday owing to our shell fire. An advance was therefore made with slight opposition as far as NEUVE CHAPELLE some 3 miles Eastward	

(9 26 6) W257—976 100,000 4/12 H W V
79
3298

Instructions regarding War Diaries and Intelligence Summaries are contained in F. S. Regs., Part II. and the Staff Manual respectively. Title pages will be prepared in manuscript.

WAR DIARY
or
INTELLIGENCE SUMMARY.
(Erase heading not required.)

Army Form C. 2118.

Hour, Date, Place	Summary of Events and Information	Remarks and references to Appendices
17th	Slow progress made by the Infantry. The Coy remained with Brigade Hd Qrs at NEUVE CHAPELLE	A reinforcement of 24 men was received bringing the Coy up to strength again. Capt J J H Nation R.E & Sapper Hankinwill [?] received the Legion of Honour & the Medaille Militaire from Genl Sir H Smith Dorrien Comdg 2nd Corps on behalf of French Govt.
18th (Sunday) NEUVE CHAPELLE	The Bridging sections of the 56th & 57th Coys were brought up in anticipation of having to bridge a canal when the advance was resumed. No progress was however made today	Lt C F Nation was admitted into hospital suffering from rheumatism. 24 N.C.O's & men joined from the base bringing the Coy up to full strength
19th	A second position was reconnoitred in case of a possible retirement. About 400 yds of barbed wire was taken out to 7th Bde to put up in front of their advanced trenches at night. 20 hand grenades were taken out to the 3 battalions of the 7th Bde in the firing line (by night) & the Officers instructed in their use. Two R.E N.C.O's were left to assist if required.	
20th	Work commenced on the retired position this morning with the assistance of 400 civilian labourers. These receive 1 fr 25 per day & their rations. The position extends some 3 miles & is to consist chiefly of ordinary fire trenches with communication trenches &c & barbed wire in front. At night the company assisted in strengthening the front position at HAUPEGARDE	+9" 3' 3'6" Section of trench of retired position at NEUVE CHAPELLE. Recd 7 bicycles for the Coy

Instructions regarding War Diaries and Intelligence Summaries are contained in F.S. Regs Part II and the Staff Manual respectively. Title pages will be prepared in manuscript.

WAR DIARY or INTELLIGENCE SUMMARY.
(Erase heading not required.)

Army Form C. 2118.

Hour, Date, Place.	Summary of Events and Information.	Remarks and References to Appendices
21st NEUVE CHAPELLE	Work on retired position continued all day. At night the Coy was employed in digging in the Irish Rifles in their advanced firing line	
22nd	Work on retired position completed as far as the actual firing trenches were concerned & a certain amount of approaches were made. At 8 pm the Coy marched to HAUPEGARDE for work, but on arrival they it was ordered back again as the rear position was to be occupied before dawn. The Coy marched back & put up wire entanglements till 4.a.m when the trenches were taken over by the Inf & the Coy went into billets at RICHBOURG ST VAAST arriving there at 5.15 a.m Good work!	
23rd	Received orders that the our Infantry firing line at NEUVE CHAPELLE was to be strengthened as much as possible. Started collecting wire & pickets round our billets & took these out after dusk & put up a low wire entanglement in front of the trenches as far as the material went. Also assisted in preparing support trenches for each of the 3 battalions in the firing line. Some of our men were fired at by our	

Instructions regarding War Diaries and Intelligence Summaries are contained in F.S. Regs. Part II and the Staff Manual respectively. Title pages will be prepared in manuscript.

WAR DIARY. OR INTELLIGENCE SUMMARY.

(Erase heading not required.)

Army Form C. 2118.

Hour, Date, Place.	Summary of Events and Information.	Remarks and References to Appendices
	own Infantry mistaking the former for the enemy, there were however no casualties.	
24th.	Similar work to yesterday except that it was not possible to go out in front of the trenches on account of the firing that was going on. The material, including sand bags for head cover was however left with each battalion to put up as opportunity offered.	
25th (Sunday) RICHBOURG ST VAAST	Collected wire & posts by day. At night 2 Sections of the Coy assisted by 200 men of the S. Lancs worked at the NEUVE CHAPELLE position; making additional approach trenches from the supports to the firing line, putting up more wire entanglements & sandbag traverses, also filling in holes in the roads made by the enemy's heavy guns. Assisted in bringing away some of the wounded. A very wet night. The Coy returned from work about 3 a.m., all but 6 men who were left to work on till dawn making an end on approach trench for the R.I.R on which it was impossible to work in the open on account of Snipers. The enemy were only 150 - 200 yds away from our position in many places.	26th The Coy collected wire &c by day. Paraded at 5.30 again for night work in the front trenches but owing to continued firing it was impossible to do any work. The Coy returned to billets at 11 p.m. One Section turned out again at 4 a.m. & took wire down to the firing line but it couldn't be put up owing to the approaching dawn
27th.	The Coy commenced making wire entanglements on the afternoon on a further retired line of trenches passing just in rear of RICHBOURG, the latter line	

Instructions regarding War Diaries and Intelligence Summaries are contained in F.S. Regs Part II and the Staff Manual respectively. Title pages will be prepared in manuscript.

WAR DIARY. OR INTELLIGENCE SUMMARY.

(Erase heading not required.)

Army Form C. 2118.

Hour, Date, Place.	Summary of Events and Information.	Remarks and References to Appendices
	have been in course of preparation by gangs of civilians and by 2 Coys of Sappers & Miners for the last two days. At 8 p.m. the Coy turned out again to dig in the firing line in the front trenches. The latter had been broken by the enemy by an attack just previously. Whilst working a night attack took place in repulsing which the Coy took part. Returned to billets about 3 a.m.	
~~27th~~ 28th	Called at 8 a.m. to issue entrenching tools to the Cavalry Brigade. At 10 a.m. Ordered to take part in an attack on NEUVE CHAPELLE & to blow up or burn a house from which the old Infantry trenches could be enfiladed. Paraded 10.35 with guncotton &c, 2 Sections accompanying the Infantry in the firing line. The attack was however not successful but the two Sections made a gallant attempt on their own account to reach the house & carry out their work. The enemy's fire was however too severe. The Sections then remained with the Infantry supports for the remainder of the day under a very heavy artillery fire.	Casualties Serg' Hinton wounded Corp' Stephens killed " Swinbutts wounded Sap' Price

Instructions regarding War Diaries and Intelligence Summaries are contained in F.S. Regs. Part II and the Staff Manual respectively. Title pages will be prepared in manuscript.

WAR DIARY
OR
INTELLIGENCE SUMMARY.
(Erase heading not required.)

Army Form C. 2118.

Hour, Date, Place.	Summary of Events and Information.	Remarks and References to Appendices
29th	Collected & prepared wire entanglements by day. In the afternoon we were shelled out of our billets & moved to another farm some 500 yds away. In the evening received orders that the Brigade was to move next morning.	
30th	Marched with the 7th Bde to DOULIEU via LA COUTURE arriving at the former place about 6 p.m & going into billets.	The Brigade is supposed to have a rest after the recent hard work & heavy fighting.
31st	Marched with the 7th Bde to MERRIS & went into billets there.	

56th Co. R.E.

Date	Officers Killed	Officers Wounded	Officers Missing		Other Ranks Killed	Other Ranks Wounded	Other Ranks Missing
23. 10. 14						2	
24. 10. 14		Lt. C. G. Martin					
28. 10. 14					died of wds 1	3	—

57th Co., R.E.

Date	Officers				Other Ranks			
	Killed	Wounded	Missing		Killed	Wounded	Missing	
21. 10. 14			Lt. R.C. Wells					
23. 10. 14						1		

Works 56th Field Coy RE. Vailly Bridge.

River Aisne.

Works completed
shewn in Red

1. Pontoon bridge C-E
2. Approaches AB BC EF.
3. Foot bridge K.
4. Approaches Heavy bridge BD. HFG.

Scale 1" to 50 yards

Foot bridge River Aisne.

Lieut RE
15/Oct/14

Detail of Works

1. Pontoon bridge C-E.
This consisted of four Weldon trestles, four pontoons and one pile trestle. Width 144'. N trestle 18' from bank. Two pontoons 6' apart. Trestles launched from rafts. Built night 13/14 Sept. 6 hours, including carrying pontoons and superstructure from Presles road to site of Bridge. Trestles had extra ledgers.

2. Approaches AB BC EF
Made by 57th Coy RE. Kept in condition by 56 Coy RE.

3. Foot bridge K
Telegraph poles had been put across from the bank to the broken end of the girder. This bridge was stiffened by a trestle and a hand rail.

4. Approaches BD HFG
These approaches intended for Heavy Traffic were drained, fascined longitudinally and transversely with 15' fascines; covered with road metal and a stiff handrail erected. The road metalling was not completed.
Total length fascined 191 yards
metalled 68 yards HF.

Section of Road.

The Approaches BD FG were ramped down to a level 3' above water level – 4' depth of earth being removed near D and G

"C" Form (Duplicate). Army Form C. 2123.

MESSAGES AND SIGNALS. No. of Message

	Charges to Pay. £ s. d.	Office Stamp.
Service Instructions.		

Handed in at the DTC Office, at 3 35 p m. Received here at 3 40 p m.

TO 56 Co. R.E.

Sender's Number.	Day of Month.	In reply to Number.	AAA
	1st		

Be ready to move your whole Companies after dark tonight aaa 56 Co take the 6 pontoon wagons with it aaa Division is going into General reserve

FROM C.R.E.

PLACE

TIME

W. 5375—423. 75,000 Pads—12/12—B. & F.—Forms/C.2123/1.

3rd Division 121/2599 D.F.W. MT.2.

56th Field Coy RE.

Vol IV. 1–30.11.14

Instructions regarding War Diaries and Intelligence Summaries are contained in F. S. Regs., Part II. and the Staff Manual respectively. Title pages will be prepared in manuscript.

WAR DIARY
or
INTELLIGENCE SUMMARY.
(*Erase heading not required.*)

Army Form C. 2118.

56th Field Co R E

Hour, Date, Place	Summary of Events and Information	Remarks and references to Appendices
1st November (Sunday) CROIX DE POPERINGE	Voluntary Church service in MERRIS, about 30 men attended. At 1 o'c. the Coy marched off again with the 7th Brigade to Croix de Poperinge ~~LOCRE~~ on Belgian frontier where it went into billets in rear of the 2nd Cavalry Division which is occupying the trenches facing the enemy	
2nd	Rest	
3rd	Ditto. Went out & examined a second line of defence for preparation in case of emergency –	
4	Rest	
5.	Commenced work on the second line of defence, making support & communication trenches for the fire trenches that had already been dug by the 17th Co R E. 7th Brigade marched off to YPRES under confidential orders, the Divnl Mounted Troops, Sectn 42nd Bde Amm Col & 7th Field Ambulance were left behind under the orders of O.C 56 Co R E. Later in the afternoon the Sectn Amm Col recd orders to rejoin their own unit.	

(9 26 6) W257–976 100,000 4/12 H W V 79/3298

Instructions regarding War Diaries and Intelligence Summaries are contained in F.S. Regs Part II and the Staff Manual respectively. Title pages will be prepared in manuscript.

WAR DIARY.
OR
INTELLIGENCE SUMMARY.
(Erase heading not required.)

Army Form C. 2118.

Hour, Date, Place.	Summary of Events and Information.	Remarks and References to Appendices
6th LOCRE	Collected wire & pickets for night work, but at 3 p.m. orders were received to march as soon as possible & join 3rd Div H^d Qrs at Dickebusch. Marched off at 4 p.m but only got as far as LOCRE owing to the congestion of traffic, billetted there therefore for the night	
7th YPRES	Marched off at 7 a.m to join 3rd Div H^d Qrs 2 miles E of YPRES after various delays, orders & counter orders finally arrived there about 9 p.m. At 4 a.m the Coy was ordered out to assist 9th Bde to strengthen their firing line, a part of which had been driven in by the enemy, finally returning to very indifferent billets at 8 a.m	
8th (Sunday)	Paraded for night work in the 7th Bde trenches at 4.30 p.m Constructed about 50 yds of fire trench, 30 yds of communication trench & about 20 yds of support trench. Also commenced a closed work about 50 yds in rear of the firing line to act as a Point d'appui. Returned to billets 1 a.m	
9th	Paraded for night work at 4.30 p.m. Completed the the Point d'appui mentioned above, dug about 100 yds of fire trench & 50 yds of support ditto. Also some new wire entanglements & repaired old.	

WAR DIARY.
OR
INTELLIGENCE SUMMARY.
(Erase heading not required.)

Army Form C. 2118.

Instructions regarding War Diaries and Intelligence Summaries are contained in F.S. Regs Part II and the Staff Manual respectively. Title pages will be prepared in manuscript.

Hour, Date, Place.	Summary of Events and Information.	Remarks and References to Appendices
10th Nov	Resting by day. Worked in the fire trenches by night, repairing & improving wire entanglements &c	
11th	The Germans made a determined attack to break through our lines commencing about 7 a.m. A portion of our firing line was forced back. The 56th Co R.E. was moved up to 9th Bde H.d Qrs at 4 p.m. to act as Infantry in support of that Brigade should the attack be further pushed. One section under Lt Leventhorpe was sent out to dig trenches in the firing line about 3 a.m. The Coy returned to billets at 6 a.m.	Lt Leventhorpe slightly wounded in left arm
12th YPRES	The Coy worked in the front trenches from 1 p.m to 8 p.m, preparing new trenches & a point d'appui some 100 yds in rear for the 9th Bde. There were 3 casualties proceeding to the work & 5 more whilst working. Billets had to be vacated again owing to heavy shell fire, the Coy is now bivouacked in an open field. Weather very cold	8 Men wounded
13th	The Coy worked in the front trenches of the 9th Bde from 8 p.m to 6 a.m preparing new trenches & putting up wire.	Weather very bad, raining
14th	The Coy worked on the front trenches of the 7th Bde, repairing portions damaged by shell fire & restoring wire entanglements. At one point of the line the Germans had sapped up to within 15 yds. In putting out the covering party, one of them shot a German & one of the covering party was also wounded	Continuous rain, roads & trenches very muddy

Instructions regarding War Diaries and Intelligence Summaries are contained in F.S. Regs Part II and the Staff Manual respectively. Title pages will be prepared in manuscript.

WAR DIARY OR INTELLIGENCE SUMMARY.

(Erase heading not required.)

Army Form C. 2118.

Hour, Date, Place.	Summary of Events and Information.	Remarks and References to Appendices
Nov. 15th (Sunday) YPRES	Two sections of the Coy worked from 8 p.m to 3 a.m in the front trenches of the K.O.S.B Position making new communication trenches & putting up fresh wire entanglements on the flanks. Owing to shortage of Subaltern Officers in this Coy, Lt Woolner of the 17th Coy R.E has been lent for work for the next two nights	Continual rain, trenches getting full of water as soon as dug. Drainage impossible
16th	Two sections worked from 8 p.m to 6 a.m in the front trenches making new trenches & repairing wire entanglements	Ditto
17th	Only one section was required for tonight's night work for repairing wire entanglements that had been damaged by shell fire during the day. The night was fine & work uninterrupted. The section returned to billets at 4 a.m.	
18th	Made a complete new fire trench for the K.O.S.B's about 100 yds long, their original one having been considerably damaged by shell fire & bombs thrown by mortars during the day. The work took from 8 p.m to 7 a.m when the party returned to billets. One of our men was wounded by our own shrapnel whilst at work.	Names called for for dispatches following sent in Lt C. E. Moores " J. A. Lesenthorpe Sergt Hinton L Corpl Bullock " Taylor

Army Form C. 2118.

WAR DIARY.
OR
INTELLIGENCE SUMMARY.
(Erase heading not required.)

Instructions regarding War Diaries and Intelligence Summaries are contained in F.S. Regs. Part II. and the Staff Manual respectively. Title pages will be prepared in manuscript.

Hour, Date, Place.	Summary of Events and Information.	Remarks and References to Appendices
19th Nov. YPRES	Only 1 Sect. required for work in the front trenches tonight putting up wire netting as a protection against high explosive bombs thrown by mortars (experimental). Some hand grenades were issued & the Infantry instructed in their use	Rabbit netting
20th	The 3rd Division at YPRES was replaced by French Troops today, the trenches being taken over commencing at 6p.m. The company marched off at 9 p.m. and arrived at WESTOUTRE 1 a.m. where it went into billets	
21st	Rest.	
22nd	Rest	
23rd	Changed billets to MONT NOIR S of WESTOUTRE	
24th	Built a siding at Ordnance Depôt WESTOUTRE, and improved the road WESTOUTRE to LOCRE (50 yards) due S of R in WESTOUTRE. Instructed officers and NCO's of the 7th Infantry Brigade in the use of handgrenades	pavé; cleared of mud and corduroy placed between bank and pavé. Jn. proceeds to England on 7 days leave

Call Neville tomorrow
Send Innes letter

Instructions regarding War Diaries and Intelligence Summaries are contained in F.S. Regs Part II and the Staff Manual respectively. Title pages will be prepared in manuscript.

WAR DIARY. OR INTELLIGENCE SUMMARY.

(Erase heading not required.)

Army Form C. 2118.

Hour, Date, Place.	Summary of Events and Information.	Remarks and References to Appendices
Nov 25th	Completed the work of the 24th. Also commenced shelters for the horses.	Huts 15' × 20'. Sunk 2' Thatched with straw
26th	One section reported to Captain Edwards for work on buildings huts for the Brigade in Reserve. Continued the shelters for the horses.	
27th 28th	The Coy was employed building huts for the Brigade in Reserve.	straw covered with twigs; dead leaves. 15' -2' -3'
29th	Two sections huts (Brigade in reserve) One section shelter for horses.	
30th	The Coy marched out to KEMMEL for 3 days work in the front trenches. At night the Coy was employed making communication trenches & connecting up the firing trenches for the Irish Rifles	Lt Moore Killed whilst working in the front trenches. Capt. Neville wounded ditto

Germans say
to within 15 yards
of firing line

Type of Redoubt
between 1st line
point d'appui

Redoubt in wood. E of YPRES.

Point d'appui behind fire trenches.

Completely surrounded: wire obstacle to trees and posts. 12' wide
12ˣ from redoubt.

Firing parapet 30 men.

16ˣ

shelter. earth mound.

A.

B.

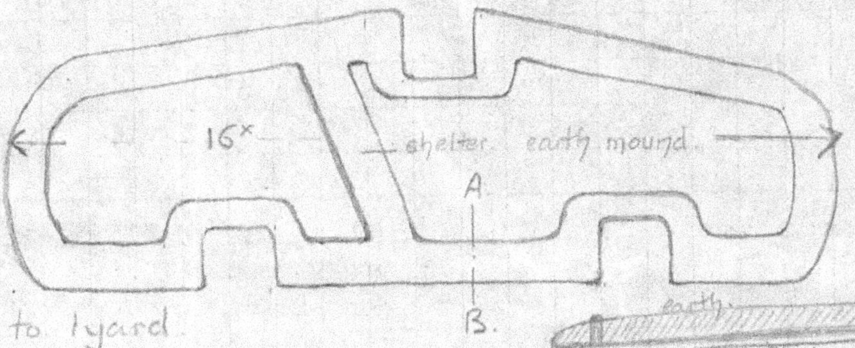

Scale. 1div to 1yard
for the plan.

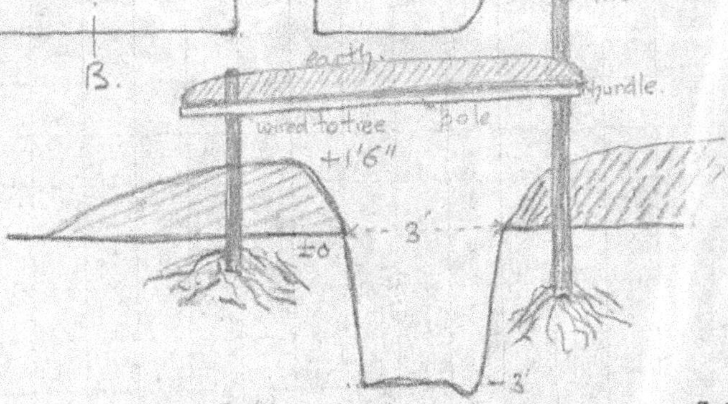

tree.

earth.

hurdle.

wired to tree

pole

+1'6"

3'

3'

Section A-B.

Dec 2nd. - Form of ready made wire entanglement.

" 10th. - Knife rest wire entanglements - not worth forwarding to M.I.T.

3rd Division

121
3944

56th Field Coy R.E.

Vol V. - 1-31.12.14

A.G.
[illegible]

Instructions regarding War Diaries and Intelligence Summaries are contained in F.S. Regs Part II and the Staff Manual respectively. Title pages will be prepared in manuscript.

WAR DIARY. OR INTELLIGENCE SUMMARY.

(Erase heading not required.)

Army Form C. 2118.

56th Co. R.E.

Hour, Date, Place.	Summary of Events and Information.	Remarks and References to Appendices
1st December — KEMMEL	Owing to the brightness of the moon it was not possible to do any work tonight in the front trenches	Lt Moores was killed last night & Capt Neville wounded by a German Sniper
2nd "	A new pattern of ready made wire entanglement was prepared during the day which was taken out to the support trenches by night & handed over to the Infantry for them to place in position as opportunity offered. These do not require to have men standing up in front of the fire trenches but can be placed in position from under cover. Some jam pot grenades were also made & taken out to the head quarters of the various regiments. The Coy returned to their old billets at Westoutre at midnight	12' – 15'; 3'; Hop pole
3rd — WESTOUTRE	The divisional arrangement at present is that each Infantry Brigade should spend 3 days in the trenches & 6 days resting. The Coy is therefore resting. The King visited the 3rd Division. The Coy lined the road & gave 3 cheers.	
4th	The Coy commenced building huts near Westoutre for some of the Infantry for whom billets cannot be found.	20'; 13; Plan; Squared timber; 18"; 3'; Section
5th	Lieut Leventhorpe proceeds to England on 7 days leave	
6th (Sunday) — MONT NOIR	Very bad weather. Some progress was made with the hutting. Hutting continued.	Lieut Oates joined the Coy. C.S.M. Palmer returned from a weeks leave in England. Sergt Bullock proceeded to England for a weeks leave

Army Form C. 2118.

WAR DIARY.
OR
INTELLIGENCE SUMMARY.
(Erase heading not required.)

Instructions regarding War Diaries and Intelligence Summaries are contained in F.S. Regs Part II and the Staff Manual respectively. Title pages will be prepared in manuscript.

Hour, Date, Place.		Summary of Events and Information.	Remarks and References to Appendices
7th Dec	WESTOUTRE	A very wet day. Work on the huts continued	
8th "		Work on huts continued. 12 huts are now completed, except for the ends	
9th "	KEMMEL	Loading up wagons in the morning. Paraded at 2.30 & proceeded by march route to KEMMEL arriving there about 6 pm to do work in the firing trenches for the 7th Inf Bde. One section sent out at night & made a shelter for the detachment of a new Trench mortar that is being brought into action 500 yds in rear of the firing line.	
10th		Collected tubs in Kemmel village for use in the fire trenches for the men to stand in to keep their feet out of the water of which there is now a great quantity in the trenches owing to continual wet weather. Collected material for and constructed a number of knife rest wire entanglements. Selected a new site for a long line of support trenches for use in case of an advance	Knife Rest Entanglement 3' 15'
11th		A very wet day & night. Repaired road in Kemmel village & carried 44 knife rest entanglements to Brigade Hd Qrs to form a store there for use in the front trenches as required.	

Instructions regarding War Diaries and Intelligence Summaries are contained in F.S. Regs. Part II. and the Staff Manual respectively. Title pages will be prepared in manuscript.

WAR DIARY. OR ~~INTELLIGENCE SUMMARY.~~

(Erase heading not required.)

Army Form C. 2118.

Hour, Date, Place.	Summary of Events and Information.	Remarks and References to Appendices
12th Dec. WESTOUTRE	Returned to Westoutre at 9.30 a.m.	Lt J.H. Richard joined the Coy. Lt J.A. Leventhorpe returned from a weeks leave in England.
13th " (Sunday)	The Coy worked on repairs to the WESTOUTRE - LOCRE Road.	
14th	An attack was delivered today in the direction of WYTSCHÆTE by the 8th Inf Bde, supported by the 9th Inf Bde, the 7th Inf Bde remaining in reserve in LOCRE. 36 German prisoners were taken.	
15th KEMMEL	The 7th Bde relieved the other two Brigades in the trenches. The Coy marched out to KEMMEL arriving there about 9 p.m. Two sections worked in the advanced trenches taking up about 50 yds of knife rest wire entanglements & putting it up in front of the Irish Rifles. 500 sandbags were issued to the Infantry.	
16th	Selected two places in the firing trenches to commence sapping & made a commencement at each progressing about 6 ft at each place. About 50 yds more of knife rest entanglement put up in front of the Irish Rifles trenches, and also about 20 or 30 yds in front of the new trench constructed after the attack on the 14th the latter under close fire from the German trenches.	
17th	Sapping continued throughout the night, working in 4 hour reliefs of 1 N.C.O. & 4 men each. Progress made 12 ft total	

Instructions regarding War Diaries and Intelligence Summaries are contained in F.S. Regs Part II and the Staff Manual respectively. Title pages will be prepared in manuscript.

WAR DIARY.
OR
INTELLIGENCE SUMMARY.
(Erase heading not required.)

Army Form C. 2118.

Hour, Date, Place.	Summary of Events and Information.	Remarks and References to Appendices
KEMMEL	Also selected 4 suitable places for building Points d'Appui (one in rear of each battalions firing line) and commenced digging on the one for the Irish Rifles (to accommodate 1 Offr & 50 men).	Capt O'Connor joined the Coy
18th	The Coy returned from KEMMEL to Billets in WESTOUTRE	A very wet day.
19th WESTOUTRE	The Coy worked on repairs to the road from WESTOUTRE to LOCRE	
20th (Sunday)	Repairs to above road continued. One party extending the horse shelters to accommodate the horses of our pontoon section which rejoined the unit from the Divl Ammn. Col. today.	Sergt White proceeds on a weeks leave to England tonight.
21st	Work on road continued also on horse shelter	Very wet afternoon, some sleet
22nd	ditto. ditto. The Cheshire Territorial Field Co R.E arrived today, one section has been attached to this Company	Wet day.
23rd	Work on road continued.	
24th KEMMEL	The Company proceeded by march route to KEMMEL arriving there about 5 p.m. Worked from 8 p.m to 1 a.m on 3 Points d'Appui behind the firing line & selected a site for a 4th one. Sapping parties continued work on the two saps that were commenced last time, but progress was very slow owing to water	Heavy Frost. A thin coat of snow on the ground

Instructions regarding War Diaries and Intelligence Summaries are contained in F.S. Regs Part II and the Staff Manual respectively. Title pages will be prepared in manuscript.

WAR DIARY. OR INTELLIGENCE SUMMARY.

(Erase heading not required.)

Army Form C. 2118.

Hour, Date, Place.		Summary of Events and Information.	Remarks and References to Appendices
25th Dec.	KEMMEL	Collecting material &c by day for night work. Night work from 8 p.m to 1 a.m on four Points d'Appui & 3 sap heads	Heavy frost.
26th "	KEMMEL	Night work as above	Thaw set in
27th " (Sunday)	WESTOUTRE	Returned to WESTOUTRE	
28th "	WESTOUTRE	Coy working on repairs to WESTOUTRE - LOCRE road. Superintending civilian working party repairing WESTOUTRE - BERTHEN Road.	A wet day
29th	WESTOUTRE	Ditto ditto as above, also started building an incinerator for the troops billeted in WESTOUTRE	Blowing a hurricane [illegible]
30th	WESTOUTRE	Ditto as above. Also started a class of pioneers 25 men from each regiment in the brigade for instruction in Revetting, trench digging, obstacles &c.	Reinforcement of 3 drivers arrived
31st	WESTOUTRE	Ditto ditto.	Reinforcement of 4 drivers arrived. A wet day

Index.........................

SUBJECT.

3RD DIV

No.	Contents.	Date.
	R. E. 56TH FIELD COY. — WAR DIARY, JAN - DEC., 1915	August missing [illegible] 4.7.21

(56,425). Wt.24,741—161. 2000. 11/20. Gp.164. A.&E.W.

3rd Division

56th Field Coy: RE.

Vol VI 1-31.1.15

Army Form C. 2118.

Instructions regarding War Diaries and Intelligence Summaries are contained in F. S. Regs., Part II. and the Staff Manual respectively. Title pages will be prepared in manuscript.

WAR DIARY

or

~~INTELLIGENCE SUMMARY.~~

(Erase heading not required.)

Hour, Date, Place	Summary of Events and Information	Remarks and References to Appendices
	56TH FIELD CO. R.E.	
	JANUARY 1915.	

(9 29 6) W 2794 100,000 8/14 H W V Forms/C. 2118/11.

Instructions regarding War Diaries and Intelligence Summaries are contained in F. S. Regs., Part II. and the Staff Manual respectively. Title pages will be prepared in manuscript.

WAR DIARY
or
INTELLIGENCE SUMMARY.
(Erase heading not required.)

Army Form C. 2118.

(1)

Hour, Date, Place	Summary of Events and Information	Remarks and References to Appendices
1st January 1915 WESTOUTRE	One section working on repair to WESTOUTRE - LOCRE Road. One Section conducting classes in fieldworks for Infantry parties of 25 men from each Battalion in the Brigade who are subsequently to work at improving the trenches in the firing line. 1 party building an Incinerator in WESTOUTRE. Superintending a party of 50 civilians working on repairs to WESTOUTRE - BERTHEN Road	Gen[l] Sir C. Fergusson assumes command of 2nd Army Corps. Gen[l] Sir H. L. Smith Dorrien assumes command of 2nd Army. A sketch of the Incinerator is appended.
2nd "	Ditto ditto as above. Sent one section under Lt Oates to KEMMEL to assist 57th Co R.E.	Capt. O'Connor accidentally wounded whilst showing Inf Officers how to throw a Tonite hand grenade. Admitted to Hosp[l]
3rd " (Sunday)	Work as above. A reinforcement of 24 sappers arrived for the Coy.	?
4th KEMMEL	The Company left for KEMMEL at 1.30 arriving there at 4 pm. Paraded for work at 5 p.m. Worked on 5 Points d'appui, making overhead cover, revetments, wire entanglement &c. The 25 Pioneers of each battalion also took up 300 sandbags each for revetments &c in the fire trenches. The 57th Co R.E. left one section behind to prepare material by day.	A map showing the positions (& lettering) of the various trenches, supporting Points, etc, is attached. The approximate positions of the German trenches are indicated in blue.

Instructions regarding War Diaries and Intelligence Summaries are contained in F. S. Regs., Part II. and the Staff Manual respectively. Title pages will be prepared in manuscript.

WAR DIARY
or
INTELLIGENCE SUMMARY.
(Erase heading not required.)

Army Form C. 2118.

(2)

Hour, Date, Place	Summary of Events and Information	Remarks and References to Appendices
5th Jan.	Collecting material by day & assisting regimental pioneers. At night each section of the Company worked on a Point d'Appui as before. The section of the 57th Co which was left behind returned to its own unit.	1 man killed & 5 wounded by shell fire at KEMMEL Cross Roads.
6th "	Work as above.	The 27th Division arrived from home & joined this army, taking over a line of trenches from left from the French.
7th "	Collecting & preparing material by day. At night an attempt was made to work on the above Points d'Appui but no progress was possible owing to the bad weather and flooded state of the ground. An attempt was also made to blow down "Lone tree" by a necklace of primers, but as the tree was 3 ft in diameter & we only had 40 primers which left a gap of about 3 ft the demolition was not successful. Carried out repairs to one of the Worcesters fire trenches as shown, to make the parapet bullet proof.	Road

HEWM 77

(9 29 6) W 2791 100,000 8/14 H W V Forms/C. 2118/11.

Instructions regarding War Diaries and Intelligence Summaries are contained in F. S. Regs., Part II. and the Staff Manual respectively. Title pages will be prepared in manuscript.

WAR DIARY
or
INTELLIGENCE SUMMARY.
(*Erase heading not required.*)

Army Form C. 2118.

(3)

Hour, Date, Place	Summary of Events and Information	Remarks and References to Appendices
8th (WESTOUTRE)	Returned to billets at WESTOUTRE in the morning. No work in the afternoon, company cleaning up & clean arm inspection.	
9th	One section bathing & fatigue duties round the billets. Two sections working on repairs to WESTOUTRE - LOCRE Road. 3 men working on the incinerator. 2 men working with a trench mortar under C.R.E. Cheshire section on road	A very wet day
10th (Sunday)	Work as above	Fine day. Lt Richard went to hospital with Influenza.
11th	One section bathing & fatigues in billets. Two sections working on the Road. Incinerator party as before. Cheshire section sent to join 57th C.R.E at KEMMEL.	Fine day. Capt Sopwith R.E joined the Coy.
12th	The Company proceeded to KEMMEL. Worked at night on S.1, S.2, S.3 Point d'Appui also on repairs to fire trenches that had fallen in from wet weather &c.	The "Comps" Company was broken up, & No 3 Section under Lt Denning rejoined this company
13th	Ditto Ditto.	

(9 29 6) W 2794 100,000 8/14 H W V Forms/C. 2118/11.

Army Form C. 2118.

(4)

Instructions regarding War Diaries and Intelligence Summaries are contained in F. S. Regs., Part II. and the Staff Manual respectively. Title pages will be prepared in manuscript.

WAR DIARY
or
INTELLIGENCE SUMMARY.
(Erase heading not required.)

Hour, Date, Place	Summary of Events and Information	Remarks and References to Appendices
14th January	Work as last two days.	1 man killed.
15th "	Ditto Ditto	1 man wounded.
16th January	Company returned to billets at WESTOUTRE. No work.	Lt. Richard returned from IP.
17th " 18th " 19th "	Work on Road, Incinerator & tarring of huts. No 1, 2 & 3 Sections each had one day's rest. Heavy snowfall on the 18th.	Notification received of the promotion of Major Nation & Capt. Richard. Following promotions were made in the Co: Cpl. Chuter to be A/Sergt; 2/Cpl Cagen to be A/Cpl; 2/Cpl. Porter A/Cpl; L/Cpl Meech to be A/2/Cpl; Spr Hadley A/Lce Cpl.
20th Wed.	Company paraded at 3 P.M. and proceeded to KEMMEL. Work (at night) as under:- 1 Section at E2 improving the parapet; 1 section at J2A revetting interior slope; 1 section at LINDENHOEK Brickfield filling sand bags with broken brick, for use in E2. Two sappers proceeded to each of the four supporting points to remain there for four days and assist with drainage, revetment, etc. Rain fell steadily all night.	 Improvement of parapet at G1.
21st Thurs.	By day the Company was employed on preparing materials for night work.	

Instructions regarding War Diaries and Intelligence Summaries are contained in F. S. Regs., Part II. and the Staff Manual respectively. Title pages will be prepared in manuscript.

WAR DIARY
or
INTELLIGENCE SUMMARY.
(Erase heading not required.)

Army Form C. 2118.

(5)

Hour, Date, Place	Summary of Events and Information	Remarks and References to Appendices
Thurs. 21st January 1915. (Continued)	Work by night as on the previous night; in addition, two sappers proceeded to G1 and assisted with improvement of parapet - vide marginal sketch on previous page. The work done at E2 was on the same principle as that at G1, but as it was impossible to drive pickets into the bottom of the trench, portable supports were made before hand - vide marginal sketch. The butt of the upright rested on the planks, hurdles etc with which the trench was littered & the pointed end was driven 6" or so into the parapet. Rain continued throughout the day and night.	
Fri. 22nd Jan.	Fine morning, slight ground frost. Work by day as before; 1 Section at LINDENHOEK, filling sand-bags; party engaged on repairing hand-carts. Work by night as before. One section under Lieut. J.A. Leventhorpe R.E. constructed a machine-gun emplacement at the left-hand end of E1 trench; this officer was shot through the head whilst completing the emplacement. The Chief Engineer, 2nd Army Corps (Major General Sandbach) visited a portion of the front line trenches (F4 and F5) and two of the supporting points (S2 and S3) between the hours of 5.30. pm and 7.30 pm. He was accompanied by a Staff Officer (Colonel Russell); Major Nation and Captain Sopwith R.E. conducted the inspecting officer round the trenches, etc. The night was fine and bright; moon in first quarter; sky slightly clouded over.	1 Officer killed.

(9 29 6) W 2794 100,000 8/14 H W V Forms/C. 2118/11.

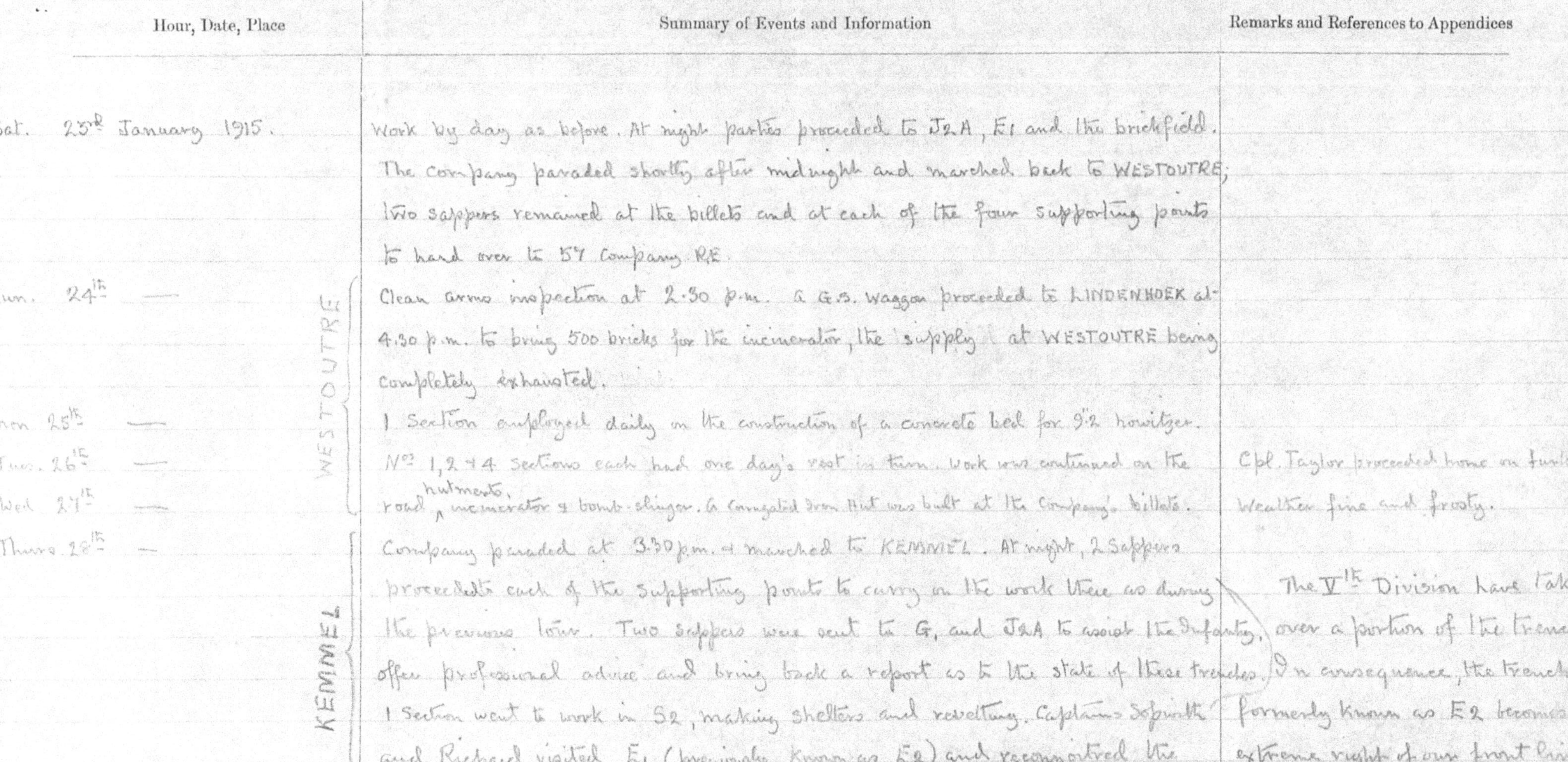

Instructions regarding War Diaries and Intelligence Summaries are contained in F. S. Regs., Part II. and the Staff Manual respectively. Title pages will be prepared in manuscript.

WAR DIARY
or
INTELLIGENCE SUMMARY.
(Erase heading not required.)

Army Form C. 2118.

(6)

Hour, Date, Place		Summary of Events and Information	Remarks and References to Appendices
Sat. 23rd January 1915.		Work by day as before. At night parties proceeded to J2A, E1 and the brickfield. The Company paraded shortly after midnight and marched back to WESTOUTRE; two sappers remained at the billets and at each of the four supporting points to hand over to 57 Company R.E.	
Sun. 24th —	WESTOUTRE	Clean arms inspection at 2.30 p.m. A G.S. Waggon proceeded to LINDENHOEK at 4.30 p.m. to bring 500 bricks for the incinerator, the supply at WESTOUTRE being completely exhausted.	
Mon 25th —	WESTOUTRE	1 Section employed daily on the construction of a concrete bed for 9.2 howitzer.	
Tues. 26th —	WESTOUTRE	Nos 1, 2 & 4 Sections each had one day's rest in turn. Work was continued on the road, hutments, incinerator & bomb-slinger. A Corrugated Iron Hut was built at the Company's billets.	Cpl. Taylor proceeded home on furlo'.
Wed 27th —	WESTOUTRE		Weather fine and frosty.
Thurs. 28th —	KEMMEL	Company paraded at 3.30 p.m. & marched to KEMMEL. At night, 2 Sappers proceeded to each of the supporting points to carry on the work there as during the previous tour. Two sappers were sent to G, and J2A to assist the Infantry, offer professional advice and bring back a report as to the state of these trenches. 1 Section went to work in S2, making shelters and revetting. Captains Sopwith and Richard visited E1 (previously known as E2) and reconnoitred the	The Vth Division have taken over a portion of the trenches. In consequence, the trench formerly known as E2 becomes the extreme right of our front line & is re-named E1.

(9 29 6) W 2794 100,000 8/14 H W V Forms/C. 2118/11.

Instructions regarding War Diaries and Intelligence Summaries are contained in F. S. Regs., Part II. and the Staff Manual respectively. Title pages will be prepared in manuscript.

WAR DIARY
or
INTELLIGENCE SUMMARY.
(Erase heading not required.)

Army Form C. 2118.

(7)

Hour, Date, Place	Summary of Events and Information	Remarks and References to Appendices
Thurs. 28th January 1915 (continued.) KEMMEL	ground with a view to deciding on a plan for defending the gaps to on either side of this trench. The night was clear, the moon nearly full; the lie of the ground could be plainly seen; the conclusions formed were discussed on the following morning with the Divisional Staff - vide infra. S1 was also visited and was found to have been greatly improved. The Worcester Regt. ~~have~~ are now in occupation of this portion of the line, having changed places with the South Lancs. Regt.	A hard frost continued throughout the day; all the ground was frozen & arrangements for drainage of trenches were consequently in abeyance.
Friday 29th —	Major Nation and Captain Sopwith met the ~~Divisional~~ G.O.C. IIIrd Division and Colonel Maurice to discuss the work required in the neighbourhood of E1. It was decided that machine-gun emplacements, covering the gaps at either end of E1, should be constructed near the Western end of the Rifle-pits and that the Rifle-pits should be extended Eastwards to connect up with E1 and provided with barbed-wire entanglements on either side. The state of the moon and the frozen nature of the ground preclude work for the present; the G.O.C. gave orders that the work ~~was~~ is to be put in hand as soon as the weather permits.	

(9 29 6) W 2794 100,000 8/14 H W V Forms/C. 2118/11.

Instructions regarding War Diaries and Intelligence Summaries are contained in F. S. Regs., Part II. and the Staff Manual respectively. Title pages will be prepared in manuscript.

WAR DIARY
or
INTELLIGENCE SUMMARY.
(*Erase heading not required.*)

Army Form C. 2118.

(8)

Hour, Date, Place	Summary of Events and Information	Remarks and References to Appendices
Friday 29th January. 1915. (continued) KEMMEL	Two sections were employed during the morning filling sand-bags at LINDENHOEK. Experiments were carried out with a new arrangement of brick-filled sand-bags with a view to preventing bullets from coming through the joints between the bags. A parapet was built to a height of 3', one sand-bag thick, the bags being laid diagonally across the parapet – i.e. midway between the positions of "header" and "stretcher". Successive layers ~~crossed one another~~ were laid at right-angles to the bags below and the whole was so disposed that each layer (in elevation) sloped downwards towards the "enemy" at about 12°. Thirty rounds were fired into this parapet; no bullets penetrated and the structure appeared quite firm + stable. This principle would be particularly useful in strengthening an existing parapet on the lines indicated on page (5) under date 21st January. By night, No 3 Section proceeded to E1 to build up "stretchers" of brick-filled sand-bags against the interior slope of the parapet, which was reported to be letting bullets through. A small party carried materials up to S2. The weather continued fine and frosty. Several 8" H.E. shells landed this day in KEMMEL village causing a number of casualties amongst the Infantry billetted there. The party stationed at S2 was increased to four sappers.	LINE OF FIRE. +4'6" +1'6" ELEVATION Minimum thickness, 7" PLAN The lower course is shown in RED. Arrangement of brick-filled sand-bags designed to avoid "straight-through" joints. Four inches of broken-brick is bullet-proof. Orders were received this day posting Capt. Richard to 26th Fd. Co. R.E. I Div.

(9 29 6) W 2794 105,000 8/14 H W V Forms/C. 2118/11.

Instructions regarding War Diaries and Intelligence Summaries are contained in F. S. Regs., Part II. and the Staff Manual respectively. Title pages will be prepared in manuscript.

WAR DIARY
or
INTELLIGENCE SUMMARY.
(Erase heading not required.)

Army Form C. 2118.

(9)

Hour, Date, Place	Summary of Events and Information	Remarks and References to Appendices
Sat. 30th January 1915 KEMMEL	The Company was employed by day in making hurdles for the revetment of second line trenches; filling sandbags; and preparing materials for night-work. At night, Major Nation and Capt. Sopwith went out with a staff officer of the IIIrd Division to select a site for a fifth supporting Point between S_4 and S_5. A party proceeded to E_1 and started work on the left-hand portion of this trench, which had hitherto been unfit for occupation; a traverse was commenced & the parapet was improved by cutting it forward & throwing the earth so obtained out to the front. Uprights for revetting the interior slope were placed in position and anchored forward by throwing over the parapet a filled sand-bag attached to the top of the upright by a ~~twisted~~ length of wire.	A party of reinforcements (1 N.C.O. and 24 Sappers) joined the Company this day. This party included one Sapper who originally came out with the Company and was sent home wounded from YPRES.
Sun. 31st —	Work as on the previous day and night. The Company marched back to WESTOUTRE after coming in from work in the trenches. Sappers were left behind, as usual, to hand over to 57 Company.	2nd Lt. R.D. Park R.E. joined the Company

(9 29 6) W 2791 100,000 8/14 H W V Forms/C. 2118/11.

INCINERATOR (FOR AN INFANTRY BRIGADE)

BUILT AT WESTOUTRE BY 56TH FIELD COMPANY R.E.

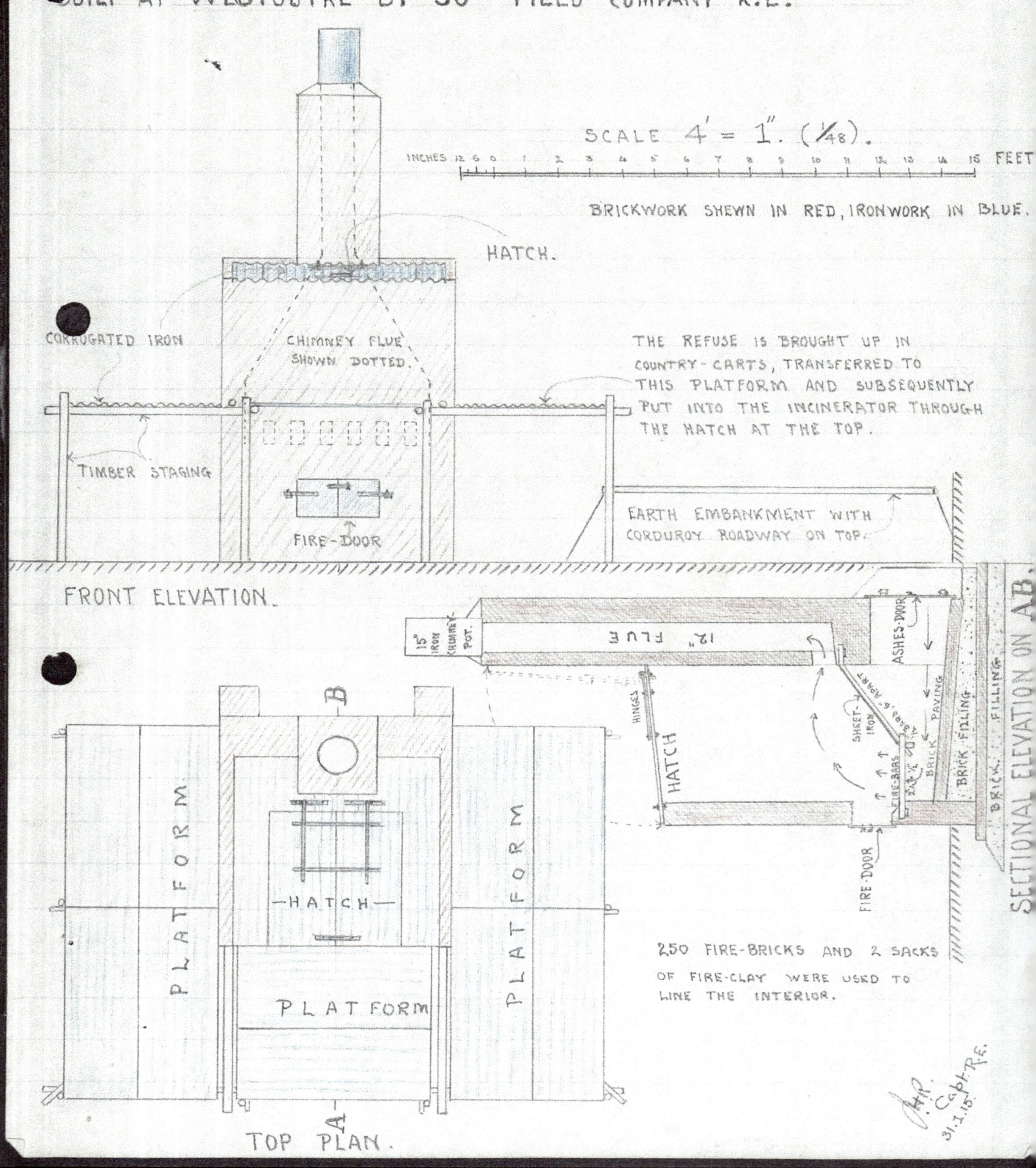

3rd Division

$\frac{121}{4586}$

56th Field Coy: RE.

Vol VII 1 – 28.2.15

Feb 12th. Boring machine tried and found useless —

Description of "Sniperscope" = a rifle in fixed position and fired after observation through attached "Periscope"

Instructions regarding War Diaries and Intelligence Summaries are contained in F. S. Regs., Part II. and the Staff Manual respectively. Title pages will be prepared in manuscript.

WAR DIARY
or
INTELLIGENCE SUMMARY.
(Erase heading not required.)

Army Form C. 2118.

Hour, Date, Place	Summary of Events and Information	Remarks and References to Appendices
MONT NOIR Feb. 1st 1915.	The company rested, and in the afternoon had a hot bath in the military bath at WESTOUTRE.	
Feb. 2nd.	No 1 Section repaired MUDDY LANE, No 2 Section practised pontooning No 3 Section continued work on 9.2" howitzer emplacement near BRULOOZE, No 4 Section practised pontooning. Details from Nos 2 & 4 Sections worked on incinerator & bath at WESTOUTRE.	
Feb. 3rd.	Nos 1 & 2 Sections practised pontooning, No 3 Section continued work as yesterday, No 4 Section repaired MUDDY LANE. Details from Nos 2 & 4 Sections worked on incinerator, and also on fitting new boring machine (for 3" bore) received today for report, after experiment.	
Feb. 4th.	No 1 Section practised pontooning No 2 Section repaired MUDDY LANE No 3 Section finished road to 9.2" howitzer emplacement & prepared foundation for laying concrete No 4 Section practised pontooning. Details (with infantry party) on incinerator. Details on making washing trough & on new boring machine experiments.	2nd Lieutenant A.R.R. Woods joined the Company.

Instructions regarding War Diaries and Intelligence Summaries are contained in F. S. Regs., Part II. and the Staff Manual respectively. Title pages will be prepared in manuscript.

WAR DIARY
or
INTELLIGENCE SUMMARY.
(Erase heading not required.)

Army Form C. 2118.

Hour, Date, Place	Summary of Events and Information	Remarks and References to Appendices
KEMMEL. Feb 5th	The Company marched to KEMMEL, parading at 3.30 pm. In the morning the CRE inspected the work done with the boring machine, & decided that boring should be continued till all the lining tubes had been used up. The work was therefore handed over to the 57th Coy for work during their period back." Captain Squire with 2nd Lt Woods reported to the GOC Brigade at LOCRE for orders as to work at KEMMEL. At night No 1 Section worked traversing support trench for G_1 & G_2. No 2 Section worked on new support point S_{4a}. No 3 Section on traversing new fire trench to cover gap between K_1 & J_3 (old trench 125x long partly dug, adopted as trench line). No 4 Section was in reserve. Major Nation with Capt Squire & 2nd Lt Woods visited S_{4a}, S_4 & portion of support trench for G_1 & G_2.	
Feb 6th.	No 1 Section worked on draining 2nd line trenches N of KEMMEL cross roads. No 2 Section (portion) wired in front of left flank of F5	

(9 29 6) W 2794 100,000 8/14 H W V Forms/C. 2118/11.

Instructions regarding War Diaries and Intelligence Summaries are contained in F. S. Regs., Part II. and the Staff Manual respectively. Title pages will be prepared in manuscript.

WAR DIARY
or
INTELLIGENCE SUMMARY.
(Erase heading not required.)

Army Form C. 2118.

Hour, Date, Place	Summary of Events and Information	Remarks and References to Appendices
	No. 3 Section filled sandbags with bricks (with additional details from No. 2) at LINDEHOEKE, No. 4 Section on S4a (revetment, floors, drainage)	
Feb 7th	No. 1 Section & No. 4 Section worked on drainage of 2nd line. No. 2 Section filled sandbags and No. 3 Section completed S4a	
Feb 8th	Captain Sopwith accompanied G.O.C. Brigade on inspection of portion of reserve line, recently taken over from 8th Brigade. Nos. 1, 2 & 3 Sections worked on drainage of choked road drains & clearing of old dug outs in this section during daylight. No. 4 Section did repairs to S3	Corporal Heath returned from leave to England.
Feb. 9th.	Nos. ~~1, 2 & 3~~ 4th Sections worked on improving drainage of portion of reserve line N. of the LAITERIE and then marched to billets at LA CLYTTE. Nos. 1, 2 & 3 Sections returned to billets at MONT NOIR. The men of these latter sections were enabled to use the bath at WESTOUTRE in the afternoon. Captain Sopwith accompanied	Corporal Warren departed on leave to England.

(9 29 6) W 2794 100,000 8/14 H W V Forms/C. 2118/11.

Army Form C. 2118.

Instructions regarding War Diaries and Intelligence Summaries are contained in F. S. Regs., Part II. and the Staff Manual respectively. Title pages will be prepared in manuscript.

WAR DIARY
or
INTELLIGENCE SUMMARY.
(Erase heading not required.)

Hour, Date, Place	Summary of Events and Information	Remarks and References to Appendices
	G.O.C. Brigade, when the latter discussed the proposed slight withdrawal of a portion of the reserve line with representatives of the Division and the 9th Brigade.	* Concrete bed for 9.2" howitzer. The concrete consists of 1 of P.C. to 2 of sand, & 2 of mortar (dry) to 5 of aggregate (broken granite). The concrete has been laid and rammed in 3" layers, successive layers being commenced within a 1/4 hour of the ~~previous~~ next lower one, to ensure no joint being formed. The surface of the platform was washed with P.C. in water, and finally 1" of sand, watered, was placed on the concrete, when finished, to keep it wet. Under the concrete is a bed of dry broken stone, 6" to 18" deep.
MONT NOIR. Feb. 10th	No 1 & 2 Sections worked on repair of MUDDY LANE, No 3 Section practised pontooning, No 4 Section worked (from LA CLYTTE) on wiring of 2nd line.	
Feb. 11th	No 1 & 2 Sections repaired MUDDY LANE No 3 Section laid concrete* bed for 9.2" howitzer at BRULOOZE, No 4 Section continued wiring of 2nd line. Party worked with boring machine, another on rifle rest and periscope rifle attachment experiments.	

(9 29 6) W 2794 100,000 8/14 H W V Forms/C. 2118/11.

Instructions regarding War Diaries and Intelligence Summaries are contained in F. S. Regs., Part II. and the Staff Manual respectively. Title pages will be prepared in manuscript.

WAR DIARY
or
INTELLIGENCE SUMMARY.
(Erase heading not required.)

Army Form C. 2118.

Hour, Date, Place	Summary of Events and Information	Remarks and References to Appendices
Feb. 12th.	No 1 Section worked on repair of MUDDY LANE, also No 3 Section. No 2 Section made fascines for bed of 15" howitzer. No 4 Section worked on wiring of 2nd line. Detailed on boring machine experiments rifle rest and periscope rifle experiments. Patterns of the rifle rests and periscope rifles were shown to the G.O.C. Division in the evening, & were ordered to be tried at KEMMEL. The boring experiments were concluded after a 15' bore had been made. The apparatus was found to be defective in many ways, too light, & requiring very experienced men to work it. It appears to be of no practical value for work in the trenches & a report to this effect has been made to the CRE. (The boring plant is W.O. order No 229 Special). Illustrations of the rifle rest and of the periscope attachment to a rifle are given in the margin. These have been sent in to the Division as inventions of the week.	THE SNIPERSCOPE Periscope string eye parapet RIFLE REST FOR NIGHT FIRING Fixed Rest for Muzzle Broken brick or shingle sliding rest for breech fillet BISCUIT BOX Clamp fixing slide Box is built into parapet. Rifle sited by day and clamped. Lateral movement is given by the sliding rest, vertical movement by a wedge under the box.

Instructions regarding War Diaries and Intelligence Summaries are contained in F. S. Regs., Part II. and the Staff Manual respectively. Title pages will be prepared in manuscript.

WAR DIARY
or
INTELLIGENCE SUMMARY.
(Erase heading not required.)

Army Form C. 2118.

Hour, Date, Place	Summary of Events and Information	Remarks and References to Appendices
KEMMEL Feb. 13th.	Company marched to KEMMEL in afternoon. No 1 Section at night continued wiring of S_2, No 2 Section wired S_4, No 3 Section worked on repair of S_5, No 4 Section prepared wire & materials.	Corporal Warren returned from leave in England.
Feb. 14th.	No 1 Section prepared wire etc No 2 Section wired S_2, No 3 Section occupied S_5 during the day, cleared the trench, drained & floored it, & got it ready for re-erection of overhead cover. No 4 Section wired S_4. Owing to extreme darkness work at night was very difficult & slow.	Lt R.W. Oates proceeded on leave to England. Corporal Allen proceeded on leave to England.
Feb. 15th.	No 1 Section worked on S_2, No 2 Section on preparing materials. No 3 Section on overhead cover for S_5, No 4 Section on S_4 & S_4a. Darkness extreme, interfering with work considerably.	Sapper Morgan (No 3 Section) was severely wounded in the head while working in S_5 on 14/2/15. Sappers Fall & Civil (No 3 Section) wounded on 15/2/15 while returning from S_5.
Feb. 16th.	No 1 Section prepared materials etc No 2 Section worked on S_2, No 3 Section on S_5 No 4 Section on wiring of S_4. After work Company marched to MONT NOIR, arriving 2.30 am.	
Feb. 17th.	At 3.30 pm orders were received to return to KEMMEL, as 9th BRIGADE had been ordered to YPRES. Company arrived 7.0 pm & 57th Compy	

(9 29 6) W 2794 100,000 8/14 H W V Forms/C. 2118/11.

Army Form C. 2118.

Instructions regarding War Diaries and Intelligence Summaries are contained in F. S. Regs., Part II. and the Staff Manual respectively. Title pages will be prepared in manuscript.

WAR DIARY
or
INTELLIGENCE SUMMARY.
(Erase heading not required.)

Hour, Date, Place	Summary of Events and Information	Remarks and References to Appendices
	who had arrived also, not having accompanied the 9th BRIGADE, returned to billets at MONT NOIR by order of the CRE. At night the Company was held as infantry reserve & remained in billets.	
Feb. 18th.	No 1 Section worked on S_2. No 2 Section wiring 2nd line. No 3 Section on S_5. No 4 Section on wiring of S_4.	Details as usual in S_2.
Feb. 19th.	No 1 Section worked on wiring reserve line. No 2 Section worked on S_2. No 3 Section on S_5. No 4 Section on wiring of S_4.	Sapper Williams proceeded on leave.
Feb. 20th.	No 1 Section worked on wiring reserve line. No 2 Section on S_5. No 3 Section on wiring reserve line. No 4 Section on wiring S_4.	Corporal Allen returned from leave.
Feb. 21st.	No 1 Section worked on repairs to F_5. No 2 Section on S_5. No 3 Section rested. No 4 Section on wiring of reserve line.	~~Maj~~ Lt. Oakes returned from leave.
MONT NOIR Feb. 22nd.	Company marched from KEMMEL at 1.0 am, leaving No 2 Section to work on wiring of 2nd line (billetted at LA CLYTTE) arriving at MONT NOIR billets at 3.15 am. Company used the hot baths at WESTOUTRE in afternoon.	Major Nation proceeded on leave.

Instructions regarding War Diaries and Intelligence Summaries are contained in F. S. Regs., Part II. and the Staff Manual respectively. Title pages will be prepared in manuscript.

WAR DIARY
or
INTELLIGENCE SUMMARY.
(Erase heading not required.)

Army Form C. 2118.

Hour, Date, Place	Summary of Events and Information	Remarks and References to Appendices
Feb. 23rd.	No 1 Section made fascines for 15" howitzer emplacement at LOCRE and did some repairs in MUDDY LANE. No 2 Section on wiring 2nd line. No 3 Section completed all work on 9.2" howitzer emplacement at BRULOOZE. No 4 Section worked on huts at LOCRE. Details on rifle rests & troughs. 15 carpenters of company employed on huts at LOCRE (these men have been there for over a fortnight). A party of carpenters from 7th Infantry Brigade were arranged for, and a working party for excavation of floors etc of 100 men arranged for 25th.	Carpenters at LOCRE
Feb 24th.	No 1 Section worked in MUDDY LANE No 2 Section wiring 2nd line. Nos 3 & 4 Sections practised pontooning. Details on rifle rests & troughs, loading hop poles for KEMMEL; and 3 bridging wagons to BAILLEUL to load timber (6 horses to each wagon).	
Feb. 25th.	Heavy snow interfered with work in morning. Nos 1 & 3 Sections practised pontooning, No 2 on wiring of 2nd line, No 4 on experiments with Ammonal. Details on rifle rests, troughs. 3 bridging wagons to BAILLEUL.	Sapper Wilkinson returns from leave

(9 29 6) W 2794 100,000 8/14 H W V Forms/C. 2118/11.

Instructions regarding War Diaries and Intelligence Summaries are contained in F. S. Regs., Part II. and the Staff Manual respectively. Title pages will be prepared in manuscript.

WAR DIARY
or
INTELLIGENCE SUMMARY.

(Erase heading not required.)

Army Form C. 2118.

Hour, Date, Place	Summary of Events and Information	Remarks and References to Appendices
KEMMEL Feb. 26th.	Party from No 1 collected hop poles & sent them to LOCRE in early morning. Company marched to KEMMEL at 4.0pm. Nos 1 & 2 Sections worked on reserve line wiring No 3 on traverses in G1. No 4 Section rested. Details to S1, S2, & S3. E Section of trenches taken over again by 7th Brigade. Captain Sopwith & 2nd Lt Woods inspected S1 & Support trenches.	C.Q.M.S. Walsham proceeded on leave to England.
Feb. 27th.	At midday billets were shelled by percussion shrapnel, (3") three men wounded. Nos 1 & 2 Sections worked on reserve line wiring No 3 Section rested No 4 Section worked on traverses in G1.	2nd Corporal Allen, Lce. Corpl Bell & Sapper Stubbes were wounded by shell fire.
Feb. 28th.	No 1 Section worked on traverses in G1 also started sapping a new trench at angle (for infantry to finish). No 2 Section rested, Nos 3 & 4 Sections did wiring of reserve line. One sergeant wounded on KEMMEL WYTSCHAETE road.	Sergeant Cole wounded by bullet in the groin. Lt. C.G. Martin DSO rejoined Company on 28th.

George Sopwith Captain
O.C. 56th Fd Co RE

(9 29 6) W 2794 100,000 8/14 H W V Forms/C. 2118/11.

3rd Division

131/4939

56th Field Coy. RE

Vol VIII 1 – 31.3.15.

Instructions regarding War Diaries and Intelligence Summaries are contained in F. S. Regs., Part II. and the Staff Manual respectively. Title pages will be prepared in manuscript.

WAR DIARY
or
INTELLIGENCE SUMMARY.
(Erase heading not required.)

Army Form C. 2118.

Hour, Date, Place	Summary of Events and Information	Remarks and References to Appendices
KEMMEL March 1st 1915	No 1 Section rested, No 2 Section worked on traverses in G1, Nos 3 & 4 Sections worked on wiring of reserve line.	
2/3/15	No 1 marked out trench in E Section for supports. No 2 collected materials by day, rested at night. No 3 assisted No 1 and Commenced dug out in F 2. No 4 Commenced dug outs and completed traverses in G 1.	15 Carpenters at work on hut construction at LOCRE
3/3/15	No 1-2-4 Sect dug (6" deep) 1000x of support trenches behind E & F Sect. No 3 sect completed dug outs in G_1 - F_2.	The moon not rising till just before midnight all work before 11 pm was carried out under great difficulties owing to the darkness.
MONT NOIR 4/3/15	Paraded 2 am. marched to back billets at LE MONT NOIR arrived 5 am. No 3 Sect remained at LA CLYTTE. Inspection of mounted sections by CRE 12 noon	
5/3/15.	No 1 & 2 Sect moved into new billets and prepared site of stables. No 3 Sect wired reserve line. No 4 sect drove out to KEMMEL. Placed Infantry working party on trenches marked out 3/3/15 behind E & F Sections and then marked out 6" deep third line of support trenches. arrived in billets 3 30 am	

(9 29 6) W 2794 100,000 8/14 H W V Forms/C. 2118/11.

Instructions regarding War Diaries and Intelligence Summaries are contained in F. S. Regs., Part II. and the Staff Manual respectively. Title pages will be prepared in manuscript.

WAR DIARY
or
INTELLIGENCE SUMMARY.
(Erase heading not required.)

Army Form C. 2118

Hour, Date, Place	Summary of Events and Information	Remarks and References to Appendices
6/3/15	No 1-2. Sects commenced Stable at new billets. No 4 Sect rested. No 3 Sect placed Infantry working party on third line of supports behind E & F sects and marked out 4th line.	
	Major E. E. Barnardiston R.E. arrived to take over the Company from Major J. J. A. Mahon.	
7/3/15	No 1-2-4 Sects worked on new stables and commenced 2 huts for drivers No 4 Sect Reserve line	
8/3/15	No 1-2-4 Sects. continued work on Stables and 2 huts also repair of road from the old billet.	
9/3/15	No 1-2-4 Sections as 8/3/15 Mounted Section moved into completed huts No 3. Sect wired second line	
10/3/15	No 1-2-4 Sect continued stable and road to billet.	
	2/Lt A.D. Park left to join 2nd Field Sqdn RE	
	Lt R.W. Oates Left for hospital (sick)	
11/3/15	Company had baths at WESTOUTRE in morning. Officers of Company attended conference at LOCRE in afternoon to	

(9 29 6) W 2794 100,000 8/14 H W V Forms/C. 2118/11.

Instructions regarding War Diaries and Intelligence Summaries are contained in F. S. Regs., Part II. and the Staff Manual respectively. Title pages will be prepared in manuscript.

WAR DIARY
or
INTELLIGENCE SUMMARY.
(Erase heading not required.)

Army Form C. 2118.

Hour, Date, Place	Summary of Events and Information	Remarks and References to Appendices
	receive instructions for attack on 12th.	
12/3/15	Company marched at 0.30 am picking up No 3 Section at LA CLYTTE, & arriving at KEMMEL CROSS ROADS at 3.5 am. Nos 3 + 4 Sections attached themselves there to the WILTSHIRES and guided them to the assembly trenches. No 1 & 2 Sections similarly acted as guides to the WORCESTERS from LINDEN HOEKE. The assembly trenches were fully occupied by 3.45 am. No 2 Section (Lt. C.G. Martindale) was allotted the task of accompanying the assaulting party & making & blocking the communication trenches on the right. No 3 Section (2nd Lt B.C. DENNING) had a similar task on the left. No 1 Section (under Captain G.E. SOPWITH, the Section commander Lt OATES being sick) were allotted for the opening of communication trenches from the German trenches to E_1 & E_2, while No 4 Section (2nd Lt A.R.R. WOODS) had to open communication trench to F_4. These trenches were not to be opened out till the assaulting column had taken the front trenches & pushed	

(9 29 6) W 2794 100,000 8/14 H W V Forms/C. 2118/11.

Instructions regarding War Diaries and Intelligence Summaries are contained in F. S. Regs., Part II. and the Staff Manual respectively. Title pages will be prepared in manuscript.

WAR DIARY
or
INTELLIGENCE SUMMARY.
(Erase heading not required.)

Army Form C. 21[illegible].

Hour, Date, Place	Summary of Events and Information	Remarks and References to Appendices
	as a covering party. With Nos 2 & 3 Sections were parties of 1 officer & 12 men each, & with Nos 1 & 4 Sections was a company each. The assault was delayed till 4.10 pm owing to misty weather interfering with the artillery bombardment. The attack failed, though Lt MARTIN & 2nd Corporal SKINNER gained a footing in a German trench with their infantry party & held it till 6.30 pm. when they were ordered to retire. Nos 1 & 4 Sections did not therefore come into action. During the assault, MAJOR BARNARDISTON, who accompanied the left of the WORCESTR assaulting party, in order to determine the line to be held after taking the advanced trenches, was wounded, also LT MARTIN & 2nd LT DENNING. In addition 18 rank & file were killed & wounded.	
	The company marched back to MONT NOIR at	
13[illegible]/15	1.0 am. on the 13th, arriving at 3.30 am, & rested during the	

(9 29 6) W 2794 100,000 8/14 H W V Forms/C. 2118/11.

Army Form C. 2118.

Instructions regarding War Diaries and Intelligence Summaries are contained in F. S. Regs., Part II. and the Staff Manual respectively. Title pages will be prepared in manuscript.

WAR DIARY
or
INTELLIGENCE SUMMARY.
(Erase heading not required.)

Hour, Date, Place	Summary of Events and Information	Remarks and References to Appendices
	day.	
KEMMEL 14/3/15	Company marched to KEMMEL at 4.15 pm. Major G. E. EVANS joined the company as O.C. As infantry reliefs did not take place that night, & firing was heavy, no work was done at night.	
15/3/15	No 4 Section worked on E, a, & Sergt CHUTER & party recovered explosives &c from E_6 (left there at the time of the assault) No 1 Section worked on wiring reserve line & No 3 Section rested.	
16/3/15	Orders received at 9.45 am transferring company to 27th Div. Company returned to MONT NOIR in afternoon & packed wagons.	
17/3/15	Company marched to RENINGHELST at 10.0 am on transfer. CRE made a farewell speech, conveying praise of G.O.C. Division over work of company during assault, & gave cards from G.O.C. to Sergt CHUTER, L.Cpl DUFFY & SAPPERS McCLOSKEY, & JORDAN & PIONEER HURLEY	!!

8/14 H W V Forms/C. 2118/11.

Instructions regarding War Diaries and Intelligence Summaries are contained in F. S. Regs., Part II. and the Staff Manual respectively. Title pages will be prepared in manuscript.

WAR DIARY
or
INTELLIGENCE SUMMARY.
(Erase heading not required.)

Army Form C. 2118.

Hour, Date, Place	Summary of Events and Information	Remarks and References to Appendices
	SERGT AMPHLETT's name has also been sent in (he was killed in the assault). Company arrived at 11.30 am & settled in new billets. Nos 3 & 4 Sections went in afternoon to DICKEBUSH with 2nd Lt ARR WOODS & Capt G. B ROOKE (T.F.) attached	
RENINGHELST 18/3/15	Carpenters worked on new huts at CANADA FARM. Remainder of company cleaned up wagons, tool carts & limbers. MAJOR EVANS went to DICKEBUSH in afternoon.	
19/3/15	No 1 & 2 Sections worked on huts at CANADA INN. No 3 & 4 Sections were on re-trenchment of ST ELOI.	2nd LT A.C. BROOKS joined
20/3/15	No 1 & 2 Sections worked on huts at CANADA INN. No 3 & 4 at St ELOI	Sapper PRICE wounded
21/3/15	1 & 2 Sections went to DICKEBUSCH, Nos 3 & 4 to RENINGHELST, & did work at their respective places as on 20 3/15	
22/3/15	1 & 2 Sections at ST ELOI 3 & 4 at RENINGHELST on work	
23/3/15	3 & 4 Sections joined up at DICKEBUSCH. All company at work on ST ELOI defences.	
24/3/15 to 27	1 & 2 Sections at ST ELOI 3 & 4 worked on huts in camp	

(9 29 6) W 2794 100,000 8/14 H W V Forms/C. 2118/11.

Instructions regarding War Diaries and Intelligence Summaries are contained in F. S. Regs., Part II. and the Staff Manual respectively. Title pages will be prepared in manuscript.

Army Form C. 2118.

WAR DIARY
or
INTELLIGENCE SUMMARY.
(Erase heading not required.)

Hour, Date, Place	Summary of Events and Information	Remarks and References to Appendices
25 3/15	As on 24 3/15	Sapper TURNER wounded.
26 3/15	3 & 4 Sections at St ELOI 1 & 2 on huts in camp	
27 3/15	3 & 4 Sections at St ELOI 1 & 2 on huts in camp & Hd Qrs huts.	
28 3/15	3 & 4 Sections at St ELOI 1 & 2 on huts in camp & Hd Qrs huts.	
29 3/15	ditto ditto.	
30 3/15	1 & 2 Sections at St ELOI 3 & 4 on huts in camp & Hd Qrs huts.	Major G. F. Evans wounded.
	Captain Sopwith visited new line of 2nd Brigade with Brigade Major.	2nd Lieutenants Whitehorne & Finnimore joined.
31 3/15	1 & 2 Sections worked on wiring & retrenchment of S6. 3 & 4 Sections on huts. G.O.C. Division presented D.C.M. ribbons to Sergt Clarke & Sapper Jordan (Sergt Humphreys, who was killed, has also been awarded the D.C.M.)	

[illegible] Capt
O.C. 56th Fd Co RE
2/4/1915

(9 29 6) W 2794 100,000 8/14 H W V Forms/C. 2118/11.

3rd Division

121/5254

56th Field Coy: RE.

Vol IX 1 - 28.4.15

Instructions regarding War Diaries and Intelligence Summaries are contained in F. S. Regs., Part II. and the Staff Manual respectively. Title pages will be prepared in manuscript.

WAR DIARY

or

~~INTELLIGENCE SUMMARY.~~

(Erase heading not required.)

Army Form C. 2118.

Hour, Date, Place	Summary of Events and Information	Remarks and References to Appendices
1st April 1915	Capt A. C. Finnimore joined for duty.	
5th "	One section, Cheshire Field Coy (T) temporarily attached.	
8th "	Acting Lance Corp: Crocker S. wounded.	
9th "	1 N.C.O. and 28 sappers joined as reinforcements.	
10th "	10891 Act. Lance Corp Hawkins, T. and 24407 Sapr Scott, A. wounded.	
11th "	24407 Sapper Scott, A. died of wounds.	
14th "	18387 Acting Sergeant Brewer, A. wounded.	
15th "	" " " " died of wounds.	
19th "	2 Lieut B. F. Whitestone and 16714 Acting Corpl Meech, J. wounded.	
28th "	2 Lieut A. W. Gordon joined for duty.	

3rd Division

121/5th/25

56th Field Coy: RE

Vol X .1 — 31.5.15.

Army Form C. 2118.

Instructions regarding War Diaries and Intelligence Summaries are contained in F. S. Regs., Part II. and the Staff Manual respectively. Title pages will be prepared in manuscript.

WAR DIARY
or
~~INTELLIGENCE~~ SUMMARY.
(Erase heading not required.)

Hour, Date, Place	Summary of Events and Information	Remarks and References to Appendices
1st May 1915 Dickebusch	Capt Finnimore reconnoitred & marked out communication trench from Q3 to join the Voormezeele – P5 existing trench.	
	No 2 section worked on the Bois Carré drain.	
	No 4 " was wiring along Ballertbeek and front of Bois Carré and working on S 6a	
	Cheshire " worked on S 6b.	
	No 23389 Sapper Chiverton H wounded. 1-5-15	
2nd May " "	—"— died of wounds. 2.5.15	
	Part of No 3 section worked by day on BOIS CARRE communication trench. Remainder supervised draining of trench between S8 and S7. No 4 section worked on S 6a & wiring the wood. Cheshire section worked on S6b.	
3rd "	Same as 2nd.	
4th "	Part of No 3 section worked by day on BOIS CARRE communication trench heavy rain prevented other work.	

(9 29 6) W 2794 100,000 8/14 H W V Forms/C. 2118/11.

Instructions regarding War Diaries and Intelligence Summaries are contained in F. S. Regs., Part II. and the Staff Manual respectively. Title pages will be prepared in manuscript.

WAR DIARY
or
~~INTELLIGENCE SUMMARY.~~
(*Erase heading not required.*)

Army Form C. 2118.

Hour, Date, Place	Summary of Events and Information	Remarks and References to Appendices
5th May	Whole company wired N.E. side of BOIS CONFLUENT until dawn.	
	18441 Sapper Brand N ~~killed~~. died of wounds 6-5-15	
	Corpl LARKE (transfered) 21402 Sapper Bowell C, 22414 Offord, N wounded. 5/5/15	
6th –	Whole company carried pickets to S6a.	
7th	Nos 1, 2, & 3 Sections carried wire & pickets to CONFLUENT—CARRE Trench.	
8th	Nos 1, 2, & 3 sections (with Div cyclists) wired from BOIS CONFLUENT to S7	
	Sappers 21414 Arnold, S, 15054 Kirwan L wounded 8/5/15	
9th	No 1 Section & Cyclists wired BOIS CARRE 500x. No 2 completed wire of BOIS CONFLUENT	
	No 3 supervised digging of BALLAARTBEEK support trenches. No 4 supervised digging of CONFLUENT trenches	
	& assisted in wiring the BOIS. Cheshire Section worked on redoubt E. of VERMOOZEELE.	
	21521 Sapper Gardner B and 18849 Sapper Goldsmith B wounded. 9-5-15	
10th	No 2 Section wired N.E. side of BOIS CONFLUENT. No 4 wired CONFLUENT—CARRE	
	Cheshire section on redoubt & C.T. East of VERMOOZEELE.	
	6413 Sapper Brackley A wounded. 10/5/15 Sapper Goldsmith died of wounds 11/5/15	
	Communication trench marked out from MOATED GRANGE to BALLAARTBEEKE	
	support trenches. Dug by Infy & R.A.	

Army Form C. 2118.

Instructions regarding War Diaries and Intelligence Summaries are contained in F. S. Regs., Part II. and the Staff Manual respectively. Title pages will be prepared in manuscript.

WAR DIARY
or
~~INTELLIGENCE SUMMARY.~~
(Erase heading not required.)

Hour, Date, Place	Summary of Events and Information	Remarks and References to Appendices
11th May DICKEBUSCH	No 2 Section & Cheshire Section wired S. side of BOIS CONFLUENT. work interrupted by shelling.	
	No 4 .. .. CONFLUENT — CARRE Trench.	
12th	No 4 Section worked on S6a, Cheshires on S6b. Cyclists wired BOIS CARRE. S.W. side	
13th	Whole Company worked on ZILLEBEEKE — HILL 60 switch. At 3.15 p.m. O.C was summoned to 8th Brigade HQ. With C.R.E. V Div. he reconnoitred the whole line by daylight. Telegraphic orders to Company sent at 4.45 from 8th Brigade HQ reached 56 Co at 6.45. 3 Officers started at once & reached 8th Bde at 7.30 p.m. 56th Company marched at 7 p.m. with tools for marking trenches and for wiring, some carried & some in a forage cart. The guide provided failed to follow the vehicle track, & shortly before reaching the canal the forage cart stuck. The men proceeded, carrying both sets of tools, to 8th Bde H.Q., where after a short delay, they were found by the O.C & sent on to ZILLEBEEKE CHURCH.	
ZILLEBEEKE.	Meanwhile the O.C. & 3 officers had made a rapid reconnaissance of the ground, which none of the latter had seen before. Some trenches near pt 60 had not yet been marked at all. The night was dark and wet. About 900 working party were expected, exact numbers and regiments unknown. By 10 p.m. about 900 Infantry were congregated, but 56 Co R E had not arrived. 2Lieut Brooks took charge of parties	

(9 29 6) W 2794 100,000 8/14 H W V Forms/C. 2118/11.

Instructions regarding War Diaries and Intelligence Summaries are contained in F. S. Regs., Part II. and the Staff Manual respectively. Title pages will be prepared in manuscript.

WAR DIARY
or
~~INTELLIGENCE SUMMARY.~~
(Erase heading not required.)

Army Form C. 2118.

Hour, Date, Place	Summary of Events and Information	Remarks and References to Appendices
	working on front line in ZILLEBEEKE Village, where the trenches had been traced with tapes. Capt Finmore also attempted to place the parties upon the partially indicated trenches on the slope of Hill 60. During this manoeuvre one party of 300 discovered that it had come to the wrong rendez-vous, and departed. In consequence it became necessary to utilise No 4 & the Cheshire section as a digging party. The total number of infantry working was about 700. 120x of support trench on extreme right was not begun. No 2 section wired about 400x of trench along ZILLEBEEKE Village, chiefly utilising existing fences, hedges, etc.	X
14th May morning	The time was limited on account of the importance of getting all bodies of troops out of artillery observation before daylight. At 1.30 a.m. when the last parties were moving away, two houses in ZILLEBEEKE were found to be on fire. The village was therefore cleared with alacrity.	
	No 28591 Sapper Roberts N was wounded at ZILLEBEEKE. 13/5/15	
	The company returned to camp at 4 a.m.	

Instructions regarding War Diaries and Intelligence Summaries are contained in F. S. Regs., Part II. and the Staff Manual respectively. Title pages will be prepared in manuscript.

WAR DIARY
or
~~INTELLIGENCE~~ SUMMARY.

(*Erase heading not required.*)

Hour, Date, Place		Summary of Events and Information	Remarks and References to Appendices
14th May	ZILLEBEEKE	No 1 Section wired 220x in front of ZILLEBEEKE under adverse circumstances.	
		No 3 " " 200x of switch line on HILL 60 " more " "	
		Great difficulties were experienced in obtaining pickets.	
		Officers started 3.30 p.m. Sections at 6.30. Returned to camp 3.15 a.m.	
	DICKEBUSCHE	Cyclists thickened wire round BOIS CARRE.	
	ZILLEBEEKE	No. 12064 Sapper Whitbourn A slightly wounded. 14-5-15	
15th May.	DICKEBUSCH	No 2 and Cheshire sections superintended digging of support trenches & communications along BALLAARTBEEKE. 270x of firetrench and three communications completed.	
		No 4 Section superintended a working party of 550 in CT from ELSENVALLE to MOATED GRANGE.	
		Cyclists continued wiring of BOIS CARRE.	
16th May	"	Nos 1, 2, & 3 Sections & Cyclists carried wire & steel posts to BOIS CONFLUENT.	
17th "	"	1, 2, & 3, Sections with 600 Infy carried wire & pickets to BALLAARTBEEK support trenches.	
18th "		1, 2, & Cheshire sections & 250 Infy carried wire & pickets " " " "	
		Cyclists wired E side of BOIS CONFLUENT.	
		Sappers No. 26565 Soffe A, 13384 Smythe J. 16149 Gunn H wounded. 18/5/15	

(9 29 6) W 2794 100,000 8/14 H W V Forms/C. 2118/11.

Instructions regarding War Diaries and Intelligence Summaries are contained in F. S. Regs., Part II. and the Staff Manual respectively. Title pages will be prepared in manuscript.

WAR DIARY
or
~~INTELLIGENCE SUMMARY.~~
(Erase heading not required.)

Army Form C. 2118.

Hour, Date, Place		Summary of Events and Information	Remarks and References to Appendices
19th May.	DICKEBUSCH	No 21565 Sapper Goffe L died of wounds. 19/5/15 Wet weather made work unprofitable.	
20th ..	..	56 Co & Cyclists wired BALLARTBEER support trenches 6 Sappers supervised finishing of digging the trenches and clearing the R7 communication trench.	
21st ..	..	No 3 Section worked on BOIS CARRE communication Trench by day No 4 .. & Cheshires supervised & assisted 150 Inf. digging & improving trenches in BOIS CONFLUENT. O.C. R.S.F. conducted along R7 Com: trench by day and necessary work pointed out.	
22nd ..	..	6 Officers reconnoitred ground between ~~T7~~ & 5th Div subsidiary line. One also reconnoitred front line trenches near SQUARE WOOD, by day. No 4 Section marked out line from T7 to OOSTHOEK FARM. Cyclists wired BOIS CARRÉ. No 3 section worked on B. CARRE C.T. by day. No 18414 Sapper O'Sullivan P wounded and died of wounds 22/5/15	

(9 29 6) W 2794 100,000 8/14 H W V Forms/C. 2118/11.

Army Form C. 2118.

Instructions regarding War Diaries and Intelligence Summaries are contained in F. S. Regs., Part II. and the Staff Manual respectively. Title pages will be prepared in manuscript.

WAR DIARY
or
~~INTELLIGENCE~~ SUMMARY.
(Erase heading not required.)

Hour, Date, Place	Summary of Events and Information	Remarks and References to Appendices
23rd May 1915. DICKEBUSCH.	No 3 Section worked on BOIS CARRE Communication trench by day.	
	No 1 Section supervised party of 150 Infy making existing ditch between 23c and 24 into a fire trench. Front parapet raised sufficiently for cover, and four good traverses built. Returned to camp 3 a.m.	
	No 4 & Cheshire sections supervised construction of trench between T7 and the 5th Div Subsidiary trench with 600 Infy. 4'6" cover obtained, by trench where possible and then by building up breastwork. Returned to camp 2.30 a.m.	
	No 8963 Sapper Dustan + wounded. 22/5/15	
24th May. "	Same work as yesterday. Making traverses to breastwork & trench.	
	Cyclists wired & cleared drives in BOIS CARRE.	
25th " "	No 4 Section marked out trenches in BOIS CONFLUENT.	
	5 of No 1 Section started sap from extension of 23c.	
	Cyclists wired & cleared BOIS CARRE.	
	Capt. Fennimore R.E. slightly wounded.	
26th " "	No 3 Section worked during day on BOIS CARRE Communication Trench.	

Instructions regarding War Diaries and Intelligence Summaries are contained in F. S. Regs., Part II. and the Staff Manual respectively. Title pages will be prepared in manuscript.

WAR DIARY
or
~~INTELLIGENCE SUMMARY.~~
(Erase heading not required.)

Army Form C. 2118.

Hour, Date, Place	Summary of Events and Information	Remarks and References to Appendices
26th May 1915 (contd).	Cyclists continued clearing drives in BOIS CARRE.	
27th May 1915. DICKEBUSCH.	No 3 Section worked on Communication Trench to BOIS CARRE	
	Cyclists carried on with above clearings.	
YPRES	Reconnaissance by 3 officers carried out E. of YPRES in neighbourhood of VERLORENHOEK.	
28th YPRES	Company less ~~portion~~ mounted section marched to YPRES and billetted in huts just N.W. of that town.	
	No 1 Section improved wire in front of front trenches S. of VERLORENHOEK near the YPRES-ROULERS Railway	
	Reconnaissance for support trenches carried out in same neighbourhood.	
29th YPRES	Nos 2 3 & 4 Sections constructed above mentioned support trenches.	
30th YPRES	Nos 2 3 & 4 Sections completed above trenches.	
31st YPRES.	Whole company moved from huts into dugouts near VLAMERTINGE.	

(9 29 6) W 2794 100,000 8/14 H W V Forms/C. 2118/11.

Instructions regarding War Diaries and Intelligence Summaries are contained in F. S. Regs., Part II. and the Staff Manual respectively. Title pages will be prepared in manuscript.

WAR DIARY

or

~~INTELLIGENCE~~ SUMMARY.

(Erase heading not required.)

Army Form C. 2118.

Hour, Date, Place	Summary of Events and Information	Remarks and References to Appendices
31st May. 1915 (contd) YPRES.	At night Nos 1 & 2 Sections commenced work on the defences of HOOGE by constructing T-heads from existing trenches. Working party 5th Yorkshire Light Infantry.	
	[illegible] Capt. O.C. 56th F^d Co. R.E.	

(9 29 6) W 2794 100,000 8/14 H W V Forms/C. 2118/11.

3rd Division

121/6357

56th Field Coy RE

Vol X/XI XII June – July.

August
diary missing.

[illegible]
4-7-21

Instructions regarding War Diaries and Intelligence Summaries are contained in F. S. Regs., Part II. and the Staff Manual respectively. Title pages will be prepared in manuscript.

WAR DIARY
or
~~INTELLIGENCE SUMMARY.~~
(Erase heading not required.)

Army Form C. 2118.

Hour, Date, Place	Summary of Events and Information	Remarks and References to Appendices
31st May 1915 (contd) YPRES.	At night Nos 1 & 2 Sections commenced work on the defences of HOOGE by constructing T heads from existing trenches. Working party 5th YORKS.	Copied on to another sheet. A.O.B. ...
1st June. YPRES	Nos 1 & 2 Sections assisted by 1 Coy 2nd S. Lancs continued work on T-heads. Work curtailed by report of bombardment. Cyclists wired in front of above T heads.	
2nd " "	The whole Company assisted by Cyclists and 2 Coys of 2nd S. Lancs proceeded to HOOGE to construct two strong points N of MENIN Road. The Germans were found to be already in possession of this ground & work was impossible. Nos 2 & 4 Sections remained and made "knife-rests" which were placed across the road just W of HOOGE. Remainder of party returned to billets. Capt Wolff (R. Scots) O.C. Cyclists killed. L/Cpl Hadley slightly wounded.	

Army Form C. 2118.

Instructions regarding War Diaries and Intelligence Summaries are contained in F. S. Regs., Part II. and the Staff Manual respectively. Title pages will be prepared in manuscript.

WAR DIARY
or
INTELLIGENCE SUMMARY.
(Erase heading not required.)

Hour, Date, Place	Summary of Events and Information	Remarks and References to Appendices
3rd June YPRES.	Nos 3 & 4 Sections worked on communication trenches round HOOGE.	
	No 2 Section & party of cyclists held ready to put in a state of defence German position to be assaulted by Lincolns. This did not take place.	
	Remainder of cyclists attached to 3rd Hd Squadron for similar purpose.	
	No Sapper Ellingham wounded.	
4th " "	No 1 Section traced out 350x of fire trench in ZOUAVE WOOD, S.W. of HOOGE.	
	1 Coy 2nd S Lancs worked on communication trenches round HOOGE.	
5th " "	No 3 Section and one Company 2nd S Lancs commenced work on new fire and support trench S of HOOGE from existing Communication trench to SANCTUARY WOOD.	

Instructions regarding War Diaries and Intelligence Summaries are contained in F. S. Regs., Part II. and the Staff Manual respectively. Title pages will be prepared in manuscript.

WAR DIARY
or
~~INTELLIGENCE~~ SUMMARY.
(Erase heading not required.)

Army Form C. 2118.

Hour, Date, Place	Summary of Events and Information	Remarks and References to Appendices
6th June 1915 YPRES.	No 3 Section and 2 Coys 2nd S. Lancs continued work on support trench. Late arrival of parties permitted little work to be done.	
	Half Cyclist Coy wired ~~at~~ E face of ZOUAVE WOOD.	
7th June 1915 "	No 4 Section with party of S Lancs worked on support trench and made T heads from communication trench ZOUAVE WOOD – HOOGE.	
	Cyclists continued wiring ZOUAVE WOOD. Lt. Swains (N.F.) was wounded.	
	Reconnaissance for water supply of SANCTUARY WOOD carried out in afternoon.	
8th " "	No 4 Section marked out new communication trench from ZOUAVE WOOD to farm S of HOOGE.	
	No 1 Section constructed T heads on old communication trench.	
	No 2 Section sent out parties during afternoon and	

(9 29 6) W 2791 100,000 8/14 H W V Forms/C. 2118/11.

Instructions regarding War Diaries and Intelligence Summaries are contained in F. S. Regs., Part II. and the Staff Manual respectively. Title pages will be prepared in manuscript.

WAR DIARY
or
INTELLIGENCE SUMMARY.
(*Erase heading not required.*)

Army Form C. 2118.

Hour, Date, Place	Summary of Events and Information	Remarks and References to Appendices
8th June 1915 YPRES	evening for improving water supply in farms N of MAPLE COPSE, and for repairing road from Bridge 14 to DUMP.	
	Cyclists continued wiring ZOUAVE WOOD.	
	Casualty No. Sapper Bishop (wounded).	
9th June " "	No I. Section continued constructing T-heads off HOOGE – ZOUAVE WOOD Communication Trench.	
	No 2 Section improved road from BRIDGE 14 to 7th Bde DUMP W of SANCTUARY WOOD. Also repairs were done to pumps as day before.	
	Cyclists continued wiring ZOUAVE WOOD.	
10th June " "	No 2 Section completed above water supply & pumps.	
	No 3 Section went out to work on new communication trench East of ZOUAVE Wood. Owing to misunderstanding about working party no work was done.	
	Reconnaissance carried out for assembly trenches along	

Instructions regarding War Diaries and Intelligence Summaries are contained in F. S. Regs., Part II. and the Staff Manual respectively. Title pages will be prepared in manuscript.

WAR DIARY
or
~~INTELLIGENCE~~ SUMMARY.
(Erase heading not required.)

Army Form C. 2118.

Hour, Date, Place	Summary of Events and Information	Remarks and References to Appendices
10th June 1915 (contd). YPRES.	MENIN Road immediately W of HOOGE.	
	Cyclists wired ZOUAVE WOOD.	
	2nd S. Lancs worked on support trench S.W. of HOOGE.	
11th June " "	No I Section worked during day on bridge over moat near SE. corner of YPRES Ramparts.	
	No 2 3 & 4 went out to construct assembly trenches W of HOOGE, working party 2nd S. Lancs.	
12th June " "	No I Section completed bridge over moat.	
	No 2 3 & 4 Sections completed ~~communication~~ assembly trenches assisted by working party of 2nd S. Lancs.	
	Cyclists continued wiring ZOUAVE WOOD.	
	No Sapper Knight wounded.	
13th June " "	No I Section proceeded to work on dugouts near level crossing of ROULERS RAILWAY over MENIN ROAD but owing to shell fire were forced to give up working. Nothing was accomplished.	

(9 29 6) W 2794 100,000 8/14 H W V Forms/C. 2118/11.

Army Form C. 2118.

Instructions regarding War Diaries and Intelligence Summaries are contained in F. S. Regs., Part II. and the Staff Manual respectively. Title pages will be prepared in manuscript.

WAR DIARY
or
~~INTELLIGENCE~~ SUMMARY.
(Erase heading not required.)

Hour, Date, Place	Summary of Events and Information	Remarks and References to Appendices
13th June 1915 (cont'd) YPRES.	At night the whole company assisted by Cyclist coy. proceeded to work on these dugouts for G.O.C. 9th Bde and to construct a communication trench to a forward observing station.	
14th " "	Whole Company assisted by cyclists completed dugouts, communication trench, and observing station for G.O.C. 9th Bde.	
	No. Sapper Harley wounded.	
	No. " Thomas "	
	No. " Barnes "	
15 " "	Company moved into Ramparts near Sally Port S.E. of YPRES. Pontoon equipment also taken to Ramparts, mounted Section remain in present billets.	
	No. 4 Section mounted a guard and took over the Pontoon Bridge from Cheshire Field Coy.	

(9 29 6) W 2794 100,000 8/14 H W V Forms/C. 2118/11.

Instructions regarding War Diaries and Intelligence Summaries are contained in F. S. Regs., Part II. and the Staff Manual respectively. Title pages will be prepared in manuscript.

WAR DIARY
or
~~INTELLIGENCE SUMMARY.~~
(Erase heading not required.)

Army Form C. 2118.

Hour, Date, Place	Summary of Events and Information	Remarks and References to Appendices
16th June (1915) YPRES	Attack made on BELLEWAARDE SALIENT in morning. At night the company went up to wire in front of captured German Trenches. Owing to General confusion little work was done.	
	No 23738 Sapper Mew H. } Killed in action " 22503 " Mangan F. } " 17057 " Hurrell T. }	
	" 25277 " Ritty A. } Wounded. " 28471 " Hudson W. } " 30504 " Mace W. } " 28863 " Rayton A. } " 28815 " Taylor F. }	
	" 11000 A/L Cpl Jordan J. 23014 Sheffield J. } Suffering from 6705 Sapper Evans H. 19974 Walters W. } Gas poisoning 14582 " Morrison R. 26247 Reast E. } (Gas shells) 30913 " Gordon G. 13343 Wilkinson G. } 11613 " O'Shea C. }	

(9 29 6) W 2794 100,000 8/14 H W V Forms/C. 2118/11.

Instructions regarding War Diaries and Intelligence Summaries are contained in F. S. Regs., Part II. and the Staff Manual respectively. Title pages will be prepared in manuscript.

WAR DIARY
or
~~INTELLIGENCE~~ SUMMARY.
(Erase heading not required.)

Army Form C. 2118.

Hour, Date, Place	Summary of Events and Information	Remarks and References to Appendices
17th June 1915 YPRES.	Nos 1, 2 & 3 Sections wired captured German trenches East of Y wood and S.E. of RAILWAY WOOD near HOOGE. Cyclist party assisted. Working party of 2/ Sloanes dug communication trenches to rear. No 18082 A/L Cpl. Marsden J. Killed.	
18th " "	No 2 Section continued wiring in front of captured trenches.	
19th " "	No 3 Section worked on stables of HOOGE Chateau.	
20th " "	No 1 Section worked on stables of HOOGE Chateau and commenced Sap across MENIN Road in HOOGE.	
21st " "	No 3 Section worked on Sap across MENIN Road & No 4 Section (less Pontoon Bridge Guard) continued work on Stables of Chateau.	
22nd " "	Attack planned on strong German point near ISLAND POST. No 2 Section went up to SANCTUARY WOOD	

Instructions regarding War Diaries and Intelligence Summaries are contained in F. S. Regs., Part II. and the Staff Manual respectively. Title pages will be prepared in manuscript.

WAR DIARY

or

~~INTELLIGENCE SUMMARY~~.

(*Erase heading not required.*)

Army Form C. 2118.

Hour, Date, Place	Summary of Events and Information	Remarks and References to Appendices
22nd June 1915. YPRES	in the morning to complete communication trenches to captured points from MENIN ROAD. Attack failed and No 2 Section repaired damaged trenches & commenced breastwork across road by BULLFARM.	
	No Sapper Swan wounded.	
23rd June " "	No I Section continued work on Stables and breastwork across MENIN ROAD.	
	No III Section continued on Saps across road.	
24th " " "	Same as previous day. Also dummy assembly	
~~25th~~ do " "	Trenches laid out for Inf. Digging party	
25th " " "	Bad weather conditions prevented work.	
26th " " "	Reconnaissance made for new Communication trench from G.H.Q. switch N. of TUILERIES to trench 21. Trench dug by Suffolks at night.	

Army Form C. 2118.

Instructions regarding War Diaries and Intelligence Summaries are contained in F. S. Regs., Part II. and the Staff Manual respectively. Title pages will be prepared in manuscript.

WAR DIARY

or

~~INTELLIGENCE SUMMARY.~~

(Erase heading not required.)

Hour, Date, Place	Summary of Events and Information	Remarks and References to Appendices
26th June '15 YPRES.	No 2 Sections & part of No 4 continued work on stables and breastwork	[illegible]
	No 3 Section worked on Dummy Assembly Trenches.	[illegible]
	Cuts through MENIN ROAD west of HOOGE	[illegible]
	commenced.	2
27th June. YPRES.	No 2 Section worked at breastwork.	
	Part of No 4 Section put screening in ZOUAVE WOOD.	
	No 3 Section laid out assembly trenches and supervised	
	digging of same	
28th June "	No 1 Section & party of Northumberland Fusiliers worked	
	on above assembly trenches and cut notches in S	
	side of MENIN ROAD.	
	No 2 Section continued work on barricade.	
	Part of No 4 Section completed screening in ZOUAVE WOOD	
	All work delayed for an hour owing to Artillery fire	
29th June "	No 1 Section & party of 2 S Lancs completed all assembly trenches	
	and began 20 saps from communication trench to C1	

(9 29 6) W 2794 100,000 8/14 H W V Forms/C. 2118/11.

Instructions regarding War Diaries and Intelligence Summaries are contained in F. S. Regs., Part II. and the Staff Manual respectively. Title pages will be prepared in manuscript.

WAR DIARY
or
~~INTELLIGENCE SUMMARY.~~
(Erase heading not required.)

Army Form C. 2118.

Hour, Date, Place	Summary of Events and Information	Remarks and References to Appendices
30th June 1915. YPRES	No 3 Section went into forward billet in SANCTUARY WOOD.	
	Lt Gordon & party of 2/[illegible] worked on fire and communication trench from ZOUAVE WOOD to HENIN ROAD.	[illegible signature]
1st July '15 "	No 3 Section worked on Comm^n Trench No 2.	
2nd July '15	No 1 Section under Lt Gordon improved cuts in road, commenced sap across road and from the end of C.o towards Y wood. No 26769 Sap' Parker L. wounded seriously.	Casualties. No 26769 Sap' Parker L. wounded
	No 3 Section improved C.T.1 worked on Stables and continued work on C.T.2	
3rd July '15 "	No 3 Section worked on C.T. sap across road & Infy worked on C.T. 2; No 2 & 4 Sections went into forward billets.	5 July '15 No 1 Section under Lieut Woods repaired pontoon bridge across canal in front of SALLYPORT in YPRES.
4th " "		
5th July '15	No 3 returned to back billet in morning.	
	No 2 Section worked on Sap in C.o. behind stables & entrenchment and improved C.T. no 1.	Casualties.
	No 4 Section worked on C.T. no 2 with Infy wounded 25277 Sap' Nelly A. wounded. No 26048 Sap' Pass[illegible] A. 5th July '15	Lieutenant A.R.R. Woods killed in action

Instructions regarding War Diaries and Intelligence Summaries are contained in F. S. Regs., Part II. and the Staff Manual respectively. Title pages will be prepared in manuscript.

WAR DIARY
or
INTELLIGENCE SUMMARY.
(Erase heading not required.)

Army Form C. 2118.

Hour, Date, Place	Summary of Events and Information	Remarks and References to Appendices
5th July '15 YPRES	No 2 Section worked as on day previously.	Wounded 5th July 15
	No 4 Section worked on C.T. No 2 work was hindered	14776 Sapr Brooks J
	by rain.	24242 " Kellis J
7 6th July 15 "	Work same as previous day.	21640 " Tapley A
8 7th July 15	Work continued same as previous day.	17791 Driver Cucumbe C
	Nos 1 & 3 Sections withdrawn Brooks Came into forward	
	billet	
9 8th July '15 "	Nos 2 & 4 Sections went back into back billet.	
	Work continued on saps in Hooge & C.O by No 1 Section.	
	No 3 Section had party working on C.T.1 & C.T.2 and	
	remainder worked on saps by night. 2nd Lancs worked	
	on Commun Trench through Zouave Wood.	
	Casualties Sapr Marshall, A. No 12240	
10 9th July '15	Work continued by the same sections as on	
	previous day, on the same work	
	2nd Lancs worked on Commun Trench through	

(9 29 6) W 2794 100,000 8/14 H W V Forms/C. 2118/11.

Instructions regarding War Diaries and Intelligence Summaries are contained in F. S. Regs., Part II. and the Staff Manual respectively. Title pages will be prepared in manuscript.

WAR DIARY
or
INTELLIGENCE SUMMARY.
(Erase heading not required.)

Army Form C. 2118.

Hour, Date, Place	Summary of Events and Information	Remarks and References to Appendices
YPRES	ZOUAVE WOOD. [illegible] No 4 Sect^n laid out Redoubt	H15a
11th July '15 "	Same work as on previous day with the same sections. Lt Young laid out & put Suffolks to work on C.T. from G H Q line to Railway. No 3 & 4 Sections laid out Redoubt at H 15 d. and Infy worked on it.	
12 July '15 "	Saps continued in HOOGE by Nos 1 & 3 Sections and C.T. 1 & 2. Lt Vance continued Comm^n Trench in ZOUAVE WOOD.	
	No 2 Section (under Lt de [illegible]) & 4 Section went into Forward Billet	
13th July '15 "	Nos 1 & 3 Sections went to back billet	
	No 4 Section worked on saps in HOOGE and G.O. and on improving C.T. no 1.	
	No 2 Section worked with Inf^y on making a C.T. from C.T. no 2 to junction [illegible] and from MARSH House to C8.	
	Casualties 26142 Sap^r Sherwood, 2.	

(9 29 6) W 2794 100,000 8/14 H W V Forms/C. 2118/11.

Army Form C. 2118.

Instructions regarding War Diaries and Intelligence Summaries are contained in F. S. Regs., Part II. and the Staff Manual respectively. Title pages will be prepared in manuscript.

WAR DIARY
or
INTELLIGENCE SUMMARY.
(Erase heading not required.)

Hour, Date, Place	Summary of Events and Information	Remarks and References to Appendices
14th July '15 YPRES	No 4 Section continued work as on previous day	No 1 Section worked on redoubt at H16.D.
	No work was done at night owing to weather.	
15th July '15	Barricade in Zouave Wood continued	No 3 Section worked on Redoubt at H15.A.
	No 4 Section continued with the same work as before.	
	No 1 Section worked on redoubt at H16.D. with Infy	
	No 3 " " " " " H15A " "	
16th July '15 "	No 2 Section continued work on Saps and Communication Trenches 1.2.	
	No work was done at night owing to weather [illegible]	
	Nos 1 & 3 Sections [illegible] went up to forward billet	
17th July '15 "	Nos 2 & 4 Sections returned to back billet.	
	No 3 Section continued work on Saps in HOOGE and improved C.T.2. Two men supervised work	

(9 29 6) W 2794 100,000 8/14 H W V Forms/C. 2118/11.

Instructions regarding War Diaries and Intelligence Summaries are contained in F. S. Regs., Part II. and the Staff Manual respectively. Title pages will be prepared in manuscript.

WAR DIARY
or
INTELLIGENCE SUMMARY.
(Erase heading not required.)

Army Form C. 2118.

Hour, Date, Place	Summary of Events and Information	Remarks and References to Appendices
YPRES	on R2 and two men worked after C Tas1 work was continued on the Barricade across Zouave Wood by No 1 Section	
16th July '15 "	No 3 Section continued work as on previous day	
	No 1 Section worked on	
	No 4 Section worked on Redoubt at I 15 A	
	No 2 Section " " " " H 16 D	
17th July 15 "	No 3 Section worked till midday as previously	
	An attack was carried out on the strong Redoubt to the N.W. of HOOGE. At 7 p.m. this was blown up by mine and the Inf attacked occupying the crater & bombing up the German Trenches.	
	No 1 Section then connected the captured German Trench on the W. of the Redoubt to the E. of Island Post and No 3 Section connected the crater to the Trench N. of BULL FARM by commn	

(9 29 6) W 2794 100,000 8/14 H W V Forms/C. 2118/11.

Army Form C. 2118.

Instructions regarding War Diaries and Intelligence Summaries are contained in F. S. Regs., Part II. and the Staff Manual respectively. Title pages will be prepared in manuscript.

WAR DIARY
or
INTELLIGENCE SUMMARY.
(Erase heading not required.)

Hour, Date, Place	Summary of Events and Information	Remarks and References to Appendices
	Trenches. Killed in Action 19-7-15	
	Casualties – No 15664 A/Sgt Harlow. J.	
	14752 A/Cpl Hadley. W	
	6701 A/Cpl Bell. J	
	13779 A/Cpl Brennan. J } wounded	
	16691 A/2/Cpl Williams. [illegible] } wounded	
	33026 Sapr Bissell. J } wounded	
	32994 " Bentley. J } wounded	
	32945 " Haggar. J } wounded	
July 20th 15	Nos 1 & 3 Sections worked on captured trenches & Commn trench. Nos 2 & 4 Sectn worked on redoubt.	
July 21st 15	Nos 1 & 3 Sections worked on the same work as previous night. Nos 2 & 4 Sectn worked on redoubt.	
	Sapper and an N.C.O. of No 2 Sectn cleared cut across road at Tunnel House.	

(9 29 6) W 2794 100,000 8/14 H W V Forms/C. 2118/11.

Instructions regarding War Diaries and Intelligence Summaries are contained in F. S. Regs., Part II. and the Staff Manual respectively. Title pages will be prepared in manuscript.

WAR DIARY
or
INTELLIGENCE SUMMARY.
(Erase heading not required.)

Army Form C. 2118.

Hour, Date, Place	Summary of Events and Information	Remarks and References to Appendices
YPRES		
22nd July '15	Nos 1 & 3 Sections came into back billets in the morning. Nos 2 & 4 Sections continued work on the redoubts at H 15 a and H 16 d.	
23rd July '15	Nos 2 & 4 Sections continued work on redoubts.	
24th July '15	No 2 Section went to Billet in and worked on dug outs for grenades and bombs in the III Divn Park. No 4 Section worked on demolishing the huts of the old III Divl head quarters	
25th July '15 "	No 2 Section continued work on the dug outs. The Company moved into billets in DICKEBUSCH at .	
DICKEBUSCH 26th July '15 "	Nos. 2 & 4 Sections worked on ~~support~~ Resmolts points at H 15 a & H 16 d. Capt. Lepurth & Lt. Le Fevre went round the front line trenches.	
27th July '15 "	No 2 & 4 Sections again worked on redoubts.	

Army Form C. 2118.

Instructions regarding War Diaries and Intelligence Summaries are contained in F. S. Regs., Part II. and the Staff Manual respectively. Title pages will be prepared in manuscript.

WAR DIARY
or
INTELLIGENCE SUMMARY.
(*Erase heading not required.*)

Hour, Date, Place	Summary of Events and Information	Remarks and References to Appendices
27th July '15 DICKEBUSCH	No 2 & 4 Section worked on Redoubts.	
	Lt Le Breuse & 2nd Lt Tunnicliffe & 2nd Lt Gatkins	
	reconnoitred commun^n trench running from	
	VOORMEZEELE to St ELOI	
28th July '15	2nd Lt Brooks handed over No 1 Section to 2nd Lt Gatkins	
	and took over work on the R.E. Park	
	No 2 & 4 Section worked on Redoubts.	
29th July '15 } 30th " } 31st " }	Nos 2 & 4 Section worked on Redoubts.	
31st July '15	2nd Lt Tunnicliffe reconnoitred redoubts and prepared	
	sketches.	
		[signature] Capt O.C. 57th F^d Co RE

3rd Division

121/7599

56th Co. R.E.

~~August~~ 1915

~~September~~

Vol XIII

War Diary. 56th Field Co. RE.

September 1915.

1st & 2nd Septr. Advance sections (living in Sanctuary Wood dugouts) worked on dugouts in various support & communication trenches. Another section worked on dugouts for Brigade HQ at W. end of Zillebeke Lake.

3rd to 6th Septr. Work as before as far as shelling permitted. Some dugouts destroyed. Capt. Sopwith RE (O.C) wounded on 6th Septr. Capt. Edwards RE took command temporarily.

6th Septr. Work commenced at night on "bombardment slits" for use for assembly during the proposed attack. Work on Brigade H.Q dugouts by day.

7th Septr. Work as before.

8th Septr. Work as before. Capt. V.P. Smith RE arrived from 7th Co. and took over command of the Company.

8th – 11th Septr. Work continued nightly on bombardment slits; also on a dugout for use as an aidpost during an attack. Brigade HQ dugouts finished on the 11th. Various small works in hand also.

12th & 13th Septr. Work on slits continued. Medical dug out & communication to it finished. Permanent party

War Diary – 56th Field Co.

of six carpenters sent off for hutting work in the divisional area

14th–16th Septr. Work on slits continued. Small parties working on various dugouts part by day part by night in and about Hooge.

12th Septr. Two. M.G. emplacements commenced in ruins of Hooge village; working by night. Wooden tramway between Sanctuary Wood & Zillebeke commenced. Work on bombardment slits continued. New dugout commenced near Culvert at Hooge. One section working in R.E. Park.

18th Septr. Work on slits, M.G. emplacements, dugout, trenchboarding in new communication trenches etc by night. Section in Park by day. Lt A.W. Gordon RE wounded during the night.

19th Septr. Advance dugouts shelled and sections left them. Work interrupted by shelling.

20th Septr. M.G. emplacements at Hooge still in hand.
+ 21st Septr. One section working on tramway, another working with & supervising infantry parties 450 strong on communication and support trenches. One section working on various jobs in Park, hutting etc.

22nd Septr. MG emplacements (two) completed. Two

War Diary – 56th Field Co.

sections working on trenches with infantry parties near Hooge. Work on tramway continued and several parties worked on minor jobs.

23rd Septr Two sections in billets (Nos 2 & 4). Other sections preparing attack dumps and assisting infantry with assembly trenches etc.

24th Septr & 25th Septr. At dawn (4.20 am) the greater part of the 7th & 8th Brigades made an attack on the German positions.

Nos 1 & 3 Secns marched to Ypres ramparts 8.15 pm ~~on~~ 24th Nos 2 & 4 Secns marched to Hooge at same time. Their task was to dig certain communication trenches between our position & the German front-line after the attack was launched.

No 2 Secn were to do two trenches & had two parties of 25 ~~men~~ infantry to assist. One trench was to be near E end of "Grafton Street", the other E of "Crater". No 4 section with a party of 50 infantry were to do a trench near the Menin Road opposite the Chateau. 2nd Lt. S.V. Young & Corpl. Bagley of No 4 Secn were both killed about midnight while moving into assembly

War Diary – 56th Field Co.

trenches. Our final bombardment started 3.50 am on 25th. A very severe German bombardment directed chiefly on Hooge & the immediate neighbourhood started three minutes later. The attack did not succeed though numerous German trenches were occupied for a short time so none of the communication trenches referred to above could even be started. The sections withdrew during the day. Casualties were 1 officer killed 1 NCO killed 3 NCOs wounded 2 men missing 9 men wounded.

Nos 1 & 3 Sections left Ramparts at 7.30 pm on 25th & came up to work at restoring the Hooge trenches but little could be done owing to the congestion of troops & wounded.

The O.C Company remained with 7th Brigade H.Q. during the attack (at Half Way House) coming up to Hooge at dusk.

Sept 26th & 27th. Company in Dickebusch billets & working on various minor jobs.

Sept. 28th. Two sections worked on dugouts at Zillebeke Lake & two by night on restoration

War Diary – 56th Field Co. RE.

28th Septr. of damaged communication trenches in & near Hooge.

29th Septr. – 30th Septr. Work as before.

Throughout the month the "back" billets of the Company — ie H.Q., mounted section & usually two sections, were in huts N.W. of Dickebusch Village & half a mile from it. Advance billets for two sections were ~~at first~~ in Sanctuary Wood till 19th Septr. For one night they had temporary dugouts near Zillebeke Lake. These were shelled twice in the 24 hours. One section then took over some dugouts near 7th Brigade HQ at Zillebeke Lake & work on making dugouts there for two complete sections was commenced before the end of the month.

A list of casualties etc is attached.

War Diary – 56th Field Co. R.E.

Septr. 1915 – Appendix.

Casualties –

Capt. G.E. Sopwith RE	wounded		6.9.15
No. 26675 Sapr. Langford J.		wounded	6.9.15
No. 14199 Lce Corp. Lean A.		"	11.9.15
8690. Corpl. Duffy J.		"	21.9.15
2nd Lt. S.V. Young.		died of wounds	25.9.15
No. 23949 Corpl. Bayley F.	killed		25.9.15
12032 Sergt. Sleeman F	wounded.		25.9.15
33038 Sapr. Lowe W.	"		25.9.15
33428 Sapr. Anderson W.	"		25.9.15
31277 Pioneer. Royle G.	wounded (died later in hospital)		25.9.15
24265 Sapr. Hoy E	wounded		25.9.15
32886 Sapr. Culpan A	"		25.9.15
32879 Sapr. Legg C	"		25.9.15
26142. Sapr. Sherwood E	"		25.9.15
33497 Sapr. Bush F	"		25.9.15
24918 Lce Corp. Boyce H	"		25.9.15
34372 Sapr. Pickering E	missing		25.9.15
28454 Sapr. Peabody E	missing		25.9.15

(see next page also)

Reinforcements.

No. 34372 Sapr. Pickering E.	8.9.15.
34620 " Passey. T.	8.9.15.
34385 " Stacey F.	8.9.15.

War Diary. 56th Field Co. RE.

Sept. 1915 — Appendix (continued).

Reinforcements (cont)

No 34516	Sapr	Bowers. G	8.9.15
33053	"	Fowler T.	8.9.15
33550	"	Webster J.	8.9.15
15103	"	Southern J.	8.9.15
22835	"	Walsh A.	8.9.15
28454	"	Peabody E	8.9.15
33654	"	Leslie J.	8.9.15
24396	"	Short R	8.9.15
25294	Lce Corp.	Moar. J.	8.9.15
34454	Sapr.	Bowles A.	8.9.15
Capt V.P. Smith. RE			8.9.15
24918	Lce Corp.	Boyce A	22.9.15
34455	Sapr.	Taylor W.	22.9.15
48779	"	Mackay A.	22.9.15
44725	Pioneer	Crellin H	22.9.15
32042	Sapr.	Cordy J.	22.9.15
23665	Sapr.	Goff E.	22.9.15
Lieut Gibson J.B.			30.9.15

Casualties (cont)

No 28321	Sapr.	T. Porter.	to hospital	5.9.15
28647	"	Ramsey J.	"	18.9.15
9841	"	Wood T.	"	18.9.15
11272.	Sergt.	Burley. R.	"	26.9.15
32901	Sapr.	Hudson. F	"	30.9.15

War Diary — 56th Field Co. RE.
Septr 1915 — Appendix (contd)

Departures:-

No 29202 Sergt. Moore J. to 182nd Mining Co. 2.9.15

Promotions:—

No 8620	Duffy J.	to Sergt.	8.9.15
14721	Woods B	Corp.	8.9.15
23070	Otten H.	to 2nd Corp.	8.9.15
10973	Whale E	to Lce Corp.	8.9.15
12032	Sleeman F	to Sergt	22.9.15
23948	Bagley F	to Corp	"
25294	Moar J	to 2nd Corp.	"
21199	Low J	to Sergt	26.9.15
3754	Rose W	to Corp.	"
22471	Downing F	to Corp.	"
12064	Whitbourn A	to 2nd Corp.	"
18683	Young J.	to 2nd Corp.	"
17705	Parsons W.	to Lce Corp.	"
19548	Liddell R	to Lce Corp.	"
22615	Ingram E	to Lce Corp.	"

~~1 of 6~~ 3rd Division 3

56th Co. R.E.

Oct + Nov.

Vol. XIV

121
7779

dg7
87w
ht2
IRE

Instructions regarding War Diaries and Intelligence Summaries are contained in F. S. Regs., Part II. and the Staff Manual respectively. Title pages will be prepared in manuscript.

WAR DIARY
or
~~INTELLIGENCE SUMMARY.~~
(*Erase heading not required.*)

Army Form C. 2118.

Hour, Date, Place	Summary of Events and Information	Remarks and References to Appendices
DICKEBUSCH.		
October 1st	No 4 Secn worked at night on Upper Grafton Ch – Liverpool Scottish working party did not turn up.	
	No 3 Secn worked on Regent Ch	
	Nos 1 & 2 Secns worked on ZILLEBEEKE LAKE dug outs	
" 2nd	Nos 3 & 4 Secns worked by night on Regent Ch & Grafton Ch respectively.	
	No 1 (sowmen) moved out to dug outs in Regent Ch during the day & worked in HOOGE at night	
	No 2 Section worked in ZILLEBEEKE dug-outs	
" 3rd	No 1 Section worked at HOOGE with 50 R.F.s (on their own front line), 50 N.F.s (on new 2nd line), 50 Liverpool Scottish (on C.T.)	
	No 2 worked by day on dug-outs & on lumber reconnaissance in YPRES.	
	No 3 & 4 Secns worked on Regent Ch & ~~Up~~ Grafton Ch C.Ts respectively.	

(9 29 6) W 2794 100,000 8/14 H W V Forms/C. 2118/11.

Army Form C. 2118.

Instructions regarding War Diaries and Intelligence Summaries are contained in F. S. Regs., Part II. and the Staff Manual respectively. Title pages will be prepared in manuscript.

WAR DIARY
or
~~INTELLIGENCE SUMMARY.~~
(Erase heading not required.)

Hour, Date, Place	Summary of Events and Information	Remarks and References to Appendices
DICKEBUSCH.		
October 4th	No 1 Secn worked by night at HOOGE with 50 Liverpool Scots & 50 N.F.s, on new 2nd line trench, C.T. and clearing.	
	No 2 Secn worked on ZILLEBEEKE dug outs.	
	No 3 Secn worked with 60 S LANCS on Lower Regent St, by night	
	No 4 Secn worked by night with 120 Liverpool Scots on Upper Grafton St & MENIN RD north drain	
" 5th	No 2 Secn moved to HOOGE yesterday afternoon & worked in HOOGE at night with 50 Liverpool Scots & 50 Lincolns	
	No 3 Secn worked by day on ZILLEBEEKE dugouts	
	No 4 Secn worked on GRAFTON St C.T.	
" 6th	No 2 Secn worked by night at HOOGE with 50 Lincolns, 50 N.F.s and 50 Liv. Scots on front line trench, new second line trench, & new C.T.	
" 7th	No 2 Secn worked with 50 Lincolns, 50 N.F.s & 50 Liv.	

(9 29 6) W 2794 100,000 8/14 H W V Forms/C. 2118/11.

Instructions regarding War Diaries and Intelligence Summaries are contained in F. S. Regs., Part II, and the Staff Manual respectively. Title pages will be prepared in manuscript.

WAR DIARY
or
~~INTELLIGENCE SUMMARY.~~
(Erase heading not required.)

Army Form C. 2118.

Hour, Date, Place	Summary of Events and Information	Remarks and references to Appendices
DICKEBUSCH.		
October 7th	Sects at HOOGE on front line trenches & C.Ts; also wired part of the front line with steel posts & entanglement to the left of & in front of the stables.	
	No 3 Secn worked in Regent St part by day, part by night with S. Lancs.	
	No 4 Section worked on Grafton St by night with 120 Liverpool Scots.	
" 8th	No 3 Secn worked at HOOGE part by day, and part by night. No 4 Secn worked by night on HOOGE.	
" 9th	No 3 Secn worked at night with Infy & provided revetting & flooring party by day at HOOGE.	
	No 4 Secn do.	
10th	Nos 1 & 2 Secn worked in park. Also provided party for work at night on Light Railway & for hutting Ridge-Guard etc.	
	No 3 Secn worked at HOOGE. Part by day with Liverpool	

(9 29 6) W 2794 100,000 8/14 H W V Forms/C. 2118/11.

Instructions regarding War Diaries and Intelligence Summaries are contained in F. S. Regs., Part II. and the Staff Manual respectively. Title pages will be prepared in manuscript.

WAR DIARY
or
~~INTELLIGENCE SUMMARY.~~
(Erase heading not required.)

Army Form C. 2118.

Hour, Date, Place	Summary of Events and Information	Remarks and references to Appendices
DICKEBUSCH		
	Scottish, part by ~~day~~ night with Lincolns & Royal Fus. also on revetting.	
	No 4 Sect worked by day & night with parties of 200 So Lin. Lerb.	
October 11th.	No 1 Sect worked with 25 Lincolns & 50 Royal Fusiliers by night & 50 transport lerb under supervision of Section Commander by day	
	No 2 Secn worked in park etc.	
	No 4 Sect same as 10th	
October 12th	No 1 Sect worked part by day and part by night with Infy working parties at HOOGE	
	No 4 Section worked part by day & part by night on Grafton St revetting & flooring etc.	
13th	No 1 Sect worked by day in Co & superintended infantry at night in front trenches.	
	No 3 Section worked on new dug outs in ZILLEBEKE POND	

Instructions regarding War Diaries and Intelligence Summaries are contained in F. S. Regs., Part II. and the Staff Manual respectively. Title pages will be prepared in manuscript.

WAR DIARY
or
~~INTELLIGENCE~~ SUMMARY.
(Erase heading not required.)

Army Form C. 2118.

Hour, Date, Place	Summary of Events and Information	Remarks and references to Appendices
DICKEBUSCH.		
	No 4 Section went to work by night in GRAFTON SCR. but were interrupted by shelling.	
October 14th	No 1 Secn worked by day in C5 and with 25 N.F.s near Stables at Hooge	
	No 2 Secn worked by night on Upper Grafton St.	
	No 3 Secn " on [illegible] work in ZILLEBEKE pond bank.	
" 15th.	No 1 Secn did the same as on 14th.	Oct 15th.
	No 2 Secn worked with 50 R.F.F. on Upper Grafton St. No 3 Secn did the same as on 14th.	40335 Sapper Wilson, wounded
" 16th.	Same as above	
" 17th	No 1 Secn moved to back billets. Nos 2 & 3 Secns worked as on 16th. No 3 Secn moved into dug outs in ZILLEBEKE.	
18th.	No 2 Secn worked mostly by day in Grafton St & near the CULVERT work interrupted by shelling	

(9 29 6) W 2791 100,000 8/14 H W V Forms/C. 2118/11.

Army Form C. 2118.

Instructions regarding War Diaries and Intelligence Summaries are contained in F. S. Regs., Part II. and the Staff Manual respectively. Title pages will be prepared in manuscript.

WAR DIARY
or
~~INTELLIGENCE SUMMARY.~~
(Erase heading not required.)

Hour, Date, Place	Summary of Events and Information	Remarks and references to Appendices
DICKEBUSCH		
	No 3 Section worked by night in Hooge.	
	No 4 Secn worked on ZILLEBEKKE dug-outs & bridges near 7th Bde hqrs.	
October 19th	No 2 Secn worked by night with H.A.C. making screened way across Zouave Wood, constructing Commn trench and clearing stream, also on re constructing Grafton St.	
	No 3 Secn worked at stables & Co	
	No 4 Secn worked on ZILLEBEKKE dug-outs	
	—	
October — November.	For the next month the Coy went back with the Div n to GODEWAERSWELDE and thence WINNEZEELE on rest.	
	While on rest the Coy instructed Infy in trench digging etc and carried out pontoon drill etc.	
	—	

(9 29 6) W 2794 100,000 8/14 H W V Forms/C. 2118/11.

Instructions regarding War Diaries and Intelligence Summaries are contained in F. S. Regs., Part II. and the Staff Manual respectively. Title pages will be prepared in manuscript.

WAR DIARY
or
~~INTELLIGENCE~~ SUMMARY.

(Erase heading not required.)

Army Form C. 2118.

Hour, Date, Place	Summary of Events and Information	Remarks and references to Appendices
DICKEBUSCH ~~October~~ November 24th.	Half of No 4 Sect worked on forward dug-outs at VOORMEZEELE and half worked with one platoon of 4 S. LANCS. on revetting CONVENT LANE Commun trench.	Captain V.P. Smith R.E. wounded
	Half No 3 Section worked on forward dugouts at VOORMEZEELE and half worked with 10 men of 4 S. LANCS on Commun trench leading to BOIS CONFLUENT.	
~~October~~ 25th.	Same as 24th.	
" 26th	No 3 Section moved into forward billets in CANAL BANK	
"	Work same as 25th	
" 27th	No 3 Section worked on Commun trench leading to trench 27 with 1 Coy of 4 S. LANCS & worked on forward dug outs.	
	No 4 Section worked with 1 Coy of 4 S. LANCS on CONVENT LANE & supervised digging of a C.T. between Q1 & Q2 by R.F.s.	

(9 29 6) W 2791 100,000 8/14 H W V Forms/C. 2118/11.

Army Form C. 2118.

Instructions regarding War Diaries and Intelligence Summaries are contained in F. S. Regs., Part II. and the Staff Manual respectively. Title pages will be prepared in manuscript.

WAR DIARY
or
INTELLIGENCE SUMMARY.
(Erase heading not required.)

Hour, Date, Place	Summary of Events and Information	Remarks and references to Appendices
DICKEBUSCH.		
November 28th	No 4 Sectn worked as on 27th.	
	No 3 Sectn worked with 1 Coy of 4 S. LANCS on digging a new C.T. alongside the one leading to Trench 27 & worked on revetting by day	
" 29th	Nos 3 & 4 Sections worked as on 28th	
	No 4 Section started to continue Light Railw from its terminus near VOORMEZEELE	
" 30th.	Work same as on 29th.	

(9 29 6) W 2791 100,000 8/14 H W V Forms/C. 2118/11.

3a

56th Co. Pt.

Dec

Vol XV

Instructions regarding War Diaries and Intelligence Summaries are contained in F. S. Regs., Part II. and the Staff Manual respectively. Title pages will be prepared in manuscript.

WAR DIARY
or
INTELLIGENCE SUMMARY.
(Erase heading not required.)

56th C. R.E.

Army Form C. 2118.

Hour, Date, Place	Summary of Events and Information	Remarks and references to Appendices
DICKEBUSCH		
December 1st	No 1 Sectn worked on new C.T. to trench 27 & 28 with one Coy of 4 S. LANCS	
	No 2 Sectn worked on CONVENT LANE C.T. revetting & draining with one Coy of 4 S. LANCS.	
" 2nd	No 1 Sectn same work as 1st.	2nd.12.15
	No 2 Sectn worked on CONVENT LANE with one Coy of 4 S. LANCS. 2/Lieut Watson and 1 N.C.O. assisted L.R.B. in reconstruction of front line trenches near T₁. Light Railway was continued	2/Lieut C Gallinis R.E. wounded by shell fire
	Casualty 2/Lieut R.E. wounded.	No 83089 Spr — wounded by shell fire
" 3rd	2/Lieut. Dinsmore took charge of No 1 Sectn. Work as on 2nd	
	No 2 Sectn worked on CONVENT LANE with one Coy of 4 S. LANCS.	
	2 N.C.O.s of No 2 Sectn supervised work on T₁ & T₂	

(9 29 6) W 2794 100,000 8/14 H W V Forms/C. 2118/11.

Instructions regarding War Diaries and Intelligence Summaries are contained in F. S. Regs., Part II. and the Staff Manual respectively. Title pages will be prepared in manuscript.

WAR DIARY
or
INTELLIGENCE SUMMARY.
(Erase heading not required.)

Army Form C. 2118.

Hour, Date, Place	Summary of Events and Information	Remarks and references to Appendices
DICKEBUSCH.		
	By day & night, by L.R.B. 1 N.C.O. and 2 sappers worked with L.R.B. on T.C.Tr by day.	
December 4th	No 1 Section continued digging C.T. to trenches 27 & 28 with one Coy of 4 S. Lancs.	
	No 2 Section worked on CONVENT LANE C.T. with one Coy of 4 S. Lancs.	
	No 3 N.C.O. and men under Lt Watson assisted L.R.A. in repairing F trenches.	
	N.C.O. and 3 men of No 4 Section started on M.G. Emplacement. 2 sappers of No 2 Sectn supervised E.Y. in constructing dug out in VOORMEZEELE.	
" 5th	No 1 Section worked as on 4th. Lieut Summers went round trench 28 with R.S.L.I. officer.	
	No 2 Section worked as on 4th. Work on M.G. Emplacement was stopped by shelling. Light Rail was continued.	

(9 29 6) W 2791 100,000 8/14 H W V Forms/C. 2118/11.

Army Form C. 2118.

Instructions regarding War Diaries and Intelligence Summaries are contained in F. S. Regs., Part II. and the Staff Manual respectively. Title pages will be prepared in manuscript.

WAR DIARY
or
INTELLIGENCE SUMMARY.
(Erase heading not required.)

Hour, Date, Place	Summary of Events and Information	Remarks and references to Appendices
DICKEBUSCH.		
Dec 6th	Work as on 5th. No 3 Sect & No 4 Sect took over from No 1 & 2 respectively.	
7th	do:	
8th	do:	
9th	No 3 Sect worked as on 8th. No 4 Section worked as on 8th. 1 N.C.O. and 2 sappers worked with 10 R.F.s in T₁ trench. Lieut. Watson inspected site for bridge over BOLLAART BEKE.	
10th	Work as on 9th. Dugout in VOORMEZEELE shelled	Casualties 10th 12.15. 2 sappers & one pioneer wounded by shell fire
11th	No 3 Sectn worked as on 9th, some sappers were kept back to work on the dugouts which had fallen in owing to heavy rain. No 4 Sectn work as on 10th	Casualties 11th. 12.15 One sapper died of wounds.
12th.	No 3 Sectn — 1 NCO & 2 sappers worked with 10 R Fs in T₁ & T₂. Remainder of sectn worked on [illegible] dugouts in VOORMEZEELE. 1 NCO & 2 men of No 4 Sect worked on [illegible] with 10 R.F. by night. No 3 Sectn worked with one Coy of S Lancs in C.T. 27 1 28	a/Cpl No 15 [illegible] — wounded a/L Cpl No 13 [illegible] " by shell fire

(9 29 6) W 2791 100,000 8/14 H W V Forms/C. 2118/11.

2

Instructions regarding War Diaries and Intelligence Summaries are contained in F. S. Regs., Part II. and the Staff Manual respectively. Title pages will be prepared in manuscript.

WAR DIARY
or
INTELLIGENCE SUMMARY.
(Erase heading not required.)

Army Form C. 2118.

Hour, Date, Place	Summary of Events and Information	Remarks and references to Appendices
DICKEBUSCH.		
" Dec 13th	Work as on 12th.	
" 14th	Work as on 13th except that parties of No 4 Section worked on new M.G. emplacements near VOORMEZEELE and on light Railway	
15th	No 4 Section completed M.G. emplacements, laid 40 yds of rails and [illegible] by night. No 2 Section worked as on 14th. No 3 Section returned to back billets after work by day. No 1 Section worked on C.T. along CANAL and on clearing passage for water below LILLE bridge.	
16th	No 1 Section worked as on 15th. No 4 Section as on 15th. No 2 Section worked on new bridge over KELLAARTBEEK and on new dugouts in VOORMEZEELE.	
17th	Work as on 16th except that 2 men of No 4 Section worked on repairing CAFE BELGE – KRUISTRAAT road & a party of No 2 Section worked on ST DTEMBER POST by day.	

(9 29 6) W 2794 100,000 8/14 H W V Forms/C. 2118/11.

Army Form C. 2118.

Instructions regarding War Diaries and Intelligence Summaries are contained in F. S. Regs., Part II. and the Staff Manual respectively. Title pages will be prepared in manuscript.

WAR DIARY
or
INTELLIGENCE SUMMARY.
(Erase heading not required.)

Hour, Date, Place	Summary of Events and Information	Remarks and references to Appendices
DICKEBUSCH.		
Dec. 18th	No 1 Sect^n part worked with Inf^y on 27-28 Connection. Work Contin^d on CT along CANAL bank & on new trench which is nearly finished. 2 NCOs & 5 men worked with party of Inf^y on Bd^e Battle H.Q. No 2 Sect^n contin^d light rails & trenches on T trenches by night. Bridge over BOLLAARTBEKE contin^d & also dug outs in VOORMEZEELE	
" 19th	Work as on 18th. The sapper No 97056 wounded.	
" 20th	Work as on 19th. Work on light Rails interrupted by Shelling	
" 21st	No 1 Sect^n worked as on 20th. No 2 Sect^n worked on building parapet of T trenches with 50 Inf^y. Remainder of work as on 20th. No 4 Sect^n contin^d work on Bd^e Battle HQ with 50 Inf^y.	
22nd	No 2 Sect^n worked on T trenches with 10 Inf^y by night & by day. And in front of mine shaft by night. Light footbridge repaired over Bollaartbeke. No 1 Sect^n worked as on 21st.	

WAR DIARY
or
INTELLIGENCE SUMMARY.
(Erase heading not required.)

Army Form C. 2118.

Instructions regarding War Diaries and Intelligence Summaries are contained in F. S. Regs., Part II. and the Staff Manual respectively. Title pages will be prepared in manuscript.

Hour, Date, Place	Summary of Events and Information	Remarks and references to Appendices
DICKEBUSCH		
Nov 23rd	No 2 Sect worked as on 22nd. No 1 Sect returned to back billets. No 3 Sect worked on [illegible] C.T. No 4 Sect worked on Div Batt H.Q.	
" 24th	No 3 Sect continued working on trench & [illegible]. Revetting of 27–28 continued & emplacement started in trench 25. No 4 Sect worked as No 2 Sect on 23rd and with 50 Inf on SEPTEMBER POST.	
" 25th	Work as on 24th. No [illegible] could not work on F trenches by daylight owing to vigilant sniping by enemy.	
26th	Work as on 25th	
27th	Work as on 26th	
28th	Work as on 27th. No 2 Sect continued with work on Div Batt H.Q.	
29th	No 4 Sect continued [illegible] along LILLE ROAD. Remainder of work as on 28th. [illegible] taken up to trenches & [illegible] in lieu of [illegible]	

WAR DIARY
or
INTELLIGENCE SUMMARY.
(Erase heading not required.)

Army Form C. 2118.

Instructions regarding War Diaries and Intelligence Summaries are contained in F. S. Regs., Part II. and the Staff Manual respectively. Title pages will be prepared in manuscript.

Hour, Date, Place	Summary of Events and Information	Remarks and references to Appendices
DICKEBUSCH.		
Aug 30th	Work as on 29th. owing to direction of [illegible] no work was done on [illegible] Baths [illegible].	
" 31st	No 2 Section worked on same works as on 30th.	
	Work of No 1 Sect. as on 30th except that [illegible] was started with [illegible] party	
	Work on Divl Baths & continued.	

3rd Division

War Diaries

56th Field Coy. R.E.

January. To December

1916

3rd Divisional Engineers.

56TH FIELD COMPANY R.E.

JANUARY 1 9 1 6.

Instructions regarding War Diaries and Intelligence Summaries are contained in F. S. Regs., Part II. and the Staff Manual respectively. Title pages will be prepared in manuscript.

WAR DIARY
or
INTELLIGENCE SUMMARY.
(Erase heading not required.)

Army Form C. 2118.

Hour, Date, Place	Summary of Events and Information	Remarks and references to Appendices
DICKEBUSCH. Jan 1st.	No 2 Sectn worked with Infy on SEPTEMBER POST. Strutting, revetting & sandbagging. 1 NCO & 4 sappers worked on T trenches by night 1 NCO + 4 sappers worked on Rails by night remainder of sectn in camp getting material	
	No 1 Sectn Portion of trench damaged by shell fire on 31st was repaired small repairs to Rails carried out. Work on connecting line continued & wind vanes constructed & erected on dug outs.	
	No 3 Sectn 1 NCO + 3 sappers on Divl HQ building - Remainder of Coy worked on Camp.	
" 2nd	As on 1st except that No 2 Sectn worked on fixing Gas boxes in R trenches & No 1 Sectn Contd work on CT & D & laid out new 27 S & 28 S.	
" 3rd	Work as on 2nd except that No 1 Sectn started extn of light Rails with 12 of pioneer Batn. No 4 Sectn relieved No 3 on ~~Forward Billets~~ Divl Battle HQ.	

(9 29 6) W 2794 100,000 8/14 H W V Forms/C. 2118/11.

Instructions regarding War Diaries and Intelligence Summaries are contained in F. S. Regs., Part II. and the Staff Manual respectively. Title pages will be prepared in manuscript.

WAR DIARY
or
INTELLIGENCE SUMMARY.

(Erase heading not required.)

Army Form C. 2118.

Hour, Date, Place	Summary of Events and Information	Remarks and References to Appendices
DICKEBUSCH Jan 4th	Work as on 3rd except that No 4 Secn worked on Div'l Battle H.Q. & No 2 Secn worked on erecting iron dug outs in VOORMEZEELE.	
" 5th	No 3 Secn relieved No 1 in Forward Billets. Remainder of work the same except No 2 Secn did not work on T trenches and worked with Pioneers on CONVENT LANE and R5. No 1 Secn worked on Div'l Battle HQ.	
" 6th	Same as on 5th	
" 7th	No 3 Secn worked on revetting 27-28 Connection by night. Drain dug for 28S. Work continued on CANAL BRIDGE. By night, 27-28 continued by day & 20 CT [illegible]. Remainder same as 5th	
" 8th	Work as on 7th & No 4 Secn started work on T trenches with R.S.F.	
" 9th	No 4 Secn worked by day & night on SEPTEMBER POST.	

(9 29 6) W 2794 100,000 8/14 H W V Forms/C. 2118/11.

Instructions regarding War Diaries and Intelligence Summaries are contained in F. S. Regs., Part II. and the Staff Manual respectively. Title pages will be prepared in manuscript.

WAR DIARY
or
INTELLIGENCE SUMMARY.
(Erase heading not required.)

Army Form C. 2118.

Hour, Date, Place	Summary of Events and Information	Remarks and References to Appendices
DICKEBUSCH Jan 9th	work was done on T[illegible] which had been blown in the day before & on 23t with the RB.	
	Remainder of work as on 8th	
" 10th	As on 9th	
" 11th	work as on 10th except that T1 was worked on, the parapet had again been blown in	
" 12th	No 1 Sectn relieved No 4 Sectn bringing remainder of work as on 9th, No 2 Sectn worked on Divl Battle HQ.	
" 13th	work as on 12th	
" 14th	work as on 13th	
" 15th	Revetting 23t — T2 continued – Remainder of work as on 14th	
" 16th	do	
17th	do No 3 Sectn worked on Divl Battle HQ.	
18th	do	
19th	do Rain behind CONVENT [illegible] no 2 Sectn	

(9 29 6) W 2794 100,000 8/14 H W V Forms/C. 2118/11.

Army Form C. 2118.

WAR DIARY
or
INTELLIGENCE SUMMARY.
(Erase heading not required.)

Instructions regarding War Diaries and Intelligence Summaries are contained in F. S. Regs., Part II. and the Staff Manual respectively. Title pages will be prepared in manuscript.

Hour, Date, Place	Summary of Events and Information	Remarks and References to Appendices
DICKEBUSCH Jan 20th	Work as on 19th Nos 3 & 4 Sectn Carpenters worked on Divl Battle H.Q.	
" " 21st	Work as on 20th.	
	Nos 3 & 4 Sections worked on New Tg with 150 R.S. Carpenters on Divl Battle H.Q.	
" " 22nd	~~[illegible]~~ worked as before	
" 23rd	do.	
24th	Parties forced to work near Camp owing to dirt of wind	
25th	Work as on 23rd No 4 Sectn relieved No 2 in Forward Billets	
26th	No 2 Sectn worked as No 4 Sectn on 25th	
	Remainder of work same as 25th	
27th	No 3 Sect 2 & 3 [illegible] continued by ~~[illegible]~~ night	
	Rest continued by day	
	No 4 Sectn as on 26th	
	Nos 1 & 2 on Divl Battle H.Q.	

(9 29 6) W 2794 100,000 8/14 H W V Forms/C. 2118/11.

Army Form C. 2118.

Instructions regarding War Diaries and Intelligence Summaries are contained in F. S. Regs., Part II. and the Staff Manual respectively. Title pages will be prepared in manuscript.

WAR DIARY
or
INTELLIGENCE SUMMARY.
(Erase heading not required.)

Hour, Date, Place		Summary of Events and Information	Remarks and References to Appendices
DICKEBUSCH	Jan 28th	No 4 Sectn worked as on 27th.	
		Branch line laid from CEMETERY to main line	
		Remainder of work as on 27th	
"	" 29th	No 4 Sectn worked as on 28th. Draining T, continued	
		26 CT badly blown in by shell fire, was repaired	
		Remainder of work as on 29th	
"	" 30th	as on 29th, no work by day owing to direction	
		of wind	
"	" 31st	as on 30th.	

(9 29 6) W 2794 100,000 8/14 H W V Forms/C. 2118/11.

56TH FIELD COMPANY R.E.

FEBRUARY 1 9 1 6.

Instructions regarding War Diaries and Intelligence Summaries are contained in F. S. Regs., Part II. and the Staff Manual respectively. Title pages will be prepared in manuscript.

WAR DIARY
or
INTELLIGENCE SUMMARY.
(Erase heading not required.)

Army Form C. 2118.

Hour, Date, Place	Summary of Events and Information	Remarks and references to Appendices
DICKEBUSCH February 1st	No 2 Sectn could not work owing to direc of wind - work on Rails continued	
	No 4 Sectn worked on SEPTEMBER POST & rails, revetting T_2 & draining T.	
	Nos 1 & 2 Sectns worked on Divl Battle H.Q.	
2nd	No 2 Sectn worked on the same work as no 4 Sectn on the 1st	
	No 3 Sectn worked on the rails and with the pioneers on 2 P S and 26 CT.	
	Nos 1 & 3 Sectns worked on Divl Battle H.Q.	
3rd	No 3 Sectn worked as on 2nd.	
	No 2 Sectn as on 1st	
	No 1 Sectn worked under H Gordon on T_7 - Carpenters on huts.	
4th	No 2, No 1 & No 4 Sectns worked on T front line trenches - no Infy assisted. Part of no 1 worked	

(9 29 6) W 2794 100,000 8/14 H W V Forms/C. 2118/11.

Instructions regarding War Diaries and Intelligence Summaries are contained in F. S. Regs., Part II. and the Staff Manual respectively. Title pages will be prepared in manuscript.

WAR DIARY
or
INTELLIGENCE SUMMARY.
(Erase heading not required.)

Army Form C. 2118.

Hour, Date, Place	Summary of Events and Information	Remarks and references to Appendices
DICKEBUSCH. Feb 4th	Tr. with 80 F. Works.	
	No 3 Sectn continued on 26 CT. and 28 S and on Rails.	
" " 5th	No 3 worked as on 4th and also on gap 23–24. Nos 1 and 4 Sectns as on 4th. Part of No 2 Sectn worked on SEPTEMBER POST.	
" 6th	Packing for move on 7th, work as on 5th.	
" 7th	Mounted Portn of Coy moved to rest billet halting at HERWAERSCAPPEL [?] the night	
NORBECOURT 8th	Remainder of Coy moved back to rest area.	
	Coy carried out usual "rest" programme of drills	
" 8th – 19th	etc. in billets at chateau of NORBECOURT.	
" 19th	Coy moved back to the line on 19th, billets near OUDERDOM.	
OUDERDOM 19th – 22nd	Coy constructed billets for men etc.	
" 28th [?]	Nos 1 & 4 Sectns moved up to Forward billets in	

(9 29 6) W 2794 100,000 8/14 H W V Forms/C. 2118/11.

Instructions regarding War Diaries and Intelligence Summaries are contained in F. S. Regs., Part II. and the Staff Manual respectively. Title pages will be prepared in manuscript.

WAR DIARY
or
INTELLIGENCE SUMMARY.
(Erase heading not required.)

Army Form C. 2118.

Hour, Date, Place	Summary of Events and Information	Remarks and references to Appendices
	CANAL BANK with O.C. and Lieuts Gordon [illegible]	
Feb. 24th	Sections worked on drainage of C.T. by day and	
	digging assembly trenches into [illegible] working	
	parties by night	Casualties
25th	As on 24th, extra men of No 3 came up to	26th Feb. Cpl [illegible] wounded.
	dugouts and back sections worked from back	28th Feb.
	billets	1 Pioneer killed
26th – 29th	Work continued as above. Heavy shelling on 28th.	2 ii Cpl. Wounded.
		6 sappers "

(9 29 6) W 2791 100,000 8/14 H W V Forms/C. 2118/11.

56TH FIELD COMPANY R.E.

MARCH 1 9 1 6.

Instructions regarding War Diaries and Intelligence Summaries are contained in F. S. Regs., Part II. and the Staff Manual respectively. Title pages will be prepared in manuscript.

WAR DIARY
or
INTELLIGENCE SUMMARY.
(Erase heading not required.)

Army Form C. 2118.

Hour, Date, Place	Summary of Events and Information	Remarks and references to Appendices
OUDERDOM.		
March 1st	Lieut Finnimore and party of sappers worked on putting bridges over front line trench. Nos 1 & 4 Sectns moved up to assembly trenches for attack next morning. O.C. and Lieut Gordon & Finnimore moved to dug out in BLUFF	
" 2nd	Attack on BLUFF. Lieut. Holmes wounded. No 1 Sectn consolidated trenches taken by 1st Gordons and No 4 Sectn started repairing S.S. but could do nothing owing to shell fire and returned 11 30	March 2nd. One Lce Cpl & 1 sapper killed. One Sergeant wounded. One Cpl ". One Lce Cpl ". 2 Sappers "
3rd	Sectns remained up in dug outs and returned on morning of the 3rd. Coy returned to back billets at OUDERDOM in the evening	
4th	Coy rested in back billets	
5th	"	

(9 29 6) W 2794 100,000 8/14 H W V Forms/C. 2118/11.

Instructions regarding War Diaries and Intelligence Summaries are contained in F. S. Regs., Part II. and the Staff Manual respectively. Title pages will be prepared in manuscript.

WAR DIARY
or
INTELLIGENCE SUMMARY.
(Erase heading not required.)

Army Form C. 2118.

Hour, Date, Place	Summary of Events and Information	Remarks and references to Appendices
OUDERDOM. March 6th.	Capt Francis invalided to hospital. Lieut Gordon took over command.	
March 7th–8th.	Coy rested.	
" 9th	Nos 2 & 3 Sectns under Lieut. Finnimore moved up to forward billets	
10th–16th.	Nos 2 & 3 Sectns worked on draining HEDGEROW. WINGATE and FIRTREE LANE by day and night and on recovering 81 S.	Coy moved to DICKEBUSCH
	Nos 1 & 4 Sectns went up to forward billets to relieve Nos 2 & 3 Sectns.	
DICKEBUSCH. 17th.	No 4 Sectn worked by night on clearing and draining MAUD LANE & FIRTREE LANE Infy supervision on 81 S. 60 lengths of steel rail carried to VOORMEZEELE. No 1 Sectn worked on WINGATE & HEDGE ROW. No 2 Sectn worked by night on gap 23–24 trench & No 3 Sectn on carrying 300x of rail to VOORMEZEELE	

(9 29 6) W 2791 100,000 8/14 H W V Forms/C. 2118/11

Instructions regarding War Diaries and Intelligence Summaries are contained in F. S. Regs., Part II. and the Staff Manual respectively. Title pages will be prepared in manuscript.

WAR DIARY
or
INTELLIGENCE SUMMARY.
(Erase heading not required.)

Army Form C. 2118.

Hour, Date, Place	Summary of Events and Information	Remarks and references to Appendices
DICKEBUSCH.		
March 18th.	No 3 Sectn laid 500x of light Rails, packed and bolted, 60x laid in posn & holes dug for turn tables No 2 Sectn worked on N. end of gap in 24. about 30x of trench cleared, deepened or drained, parados & parapet built up drains dug. work continually interrupted by M.G. fire. Nos 1 & 4 Sectns worked as on 17th	
" 19th	No 3 Sectn laid 230x of Rails and put in 2 turn tables. No 2 Sectn worked on Gaps in 24 now passable by day. Nos 1 & 4 Sectns as on 17th	March 20th.
" 20th	No 3 Sectn laid 350x of rails. Nos 2, 1 & 4 Sectns work as on 19th. Large quantity of water drained off WINGATE.	Sapper wounded.
" 21	No 2 Sectn worked on Gap in 24. No 3 Sectn finished light Rails and carried	

Army Form C. 2118

Instructions regarding War Diaries and Intelligence Summaries are contained in F. S. Regs., Part II. and the Staff Manual respectively. Title pages will be prepared in manuscript.

WAR DIARY
or
INTELLIGENCE SUMMARY.
(Erase heading not required.)

Hour, Date, Place	Summary of Events and Information	Remarks and references to Appendices
DICKEBUSCH.		
	Material up to Q.	
	Nos 1 & 4 Sectns worked on Q, not much work done	March 22nd. Work as on 21st.
	owing to lack of material	
	28 dummies completed by carpenters	
March 23rd.	No 5 Sectn worked on gap in trench 24, building	
	up a traverse and parapet — work had to stop	
	10 to 11 owing to shelling and again at 11.15 when	
	heavy shells were turned on.	
	Nos 1 & 4 Sectns set out from VOORMEZEELE to work	
	on Q but owing to heavy shelling and casualties	
	to carrying party no material could be got up	
	and no work was done.	
" 24	Work as on 23rd No 2 Sectn worked instead of	
	No 3 on 24	
" 25th	No 3 Sectn worked on gap in 24.	
	Nos 1 & 4 Sectns worked on Q. Carrying up Hem	

(9 29 6) W 2791 100,000 8/14 H W V Forms/C. 2118/11.

Instructions regarding War Diaries and Intelligence Summaries are contained in F. S. Regs., Part II. and the Staff Manual respectively. Title pages will be prepared in manuscript.

WAR DIARY
or
INTELLIGENCE SUMMARY.
(Erase heading not required.)

Army Form C. 2118.

Hour, Date, Place	Summary of Events and Information	Remarks and References to Appendices
DICKEBUSCH.		
	own material	
March 26th	Nos 1&4 Sections worked on strutting R1.	
March 27th	Attack on St Eloi with mine explosions.	
	Nos 2 & 3 Sections went up to work on	
	CT to enemy captured trenches. Bombardment	
	by enemy started when Sections were in R2 and	
	continued till morning – no work done. Sectns	
	returned by front line to left.	
28th	Nos 1&3 Sections and part of No 4 worked on joining	
	up old front line to Bombing Post in front of	
	T1 – Heavy shelling continuous during night	
29th	work as on 28th. Shelling during night. Bombing	
	Post was advanced during night we cleared the	
	old 'block' and built up trench to new 'block'.	
	Lieut Gordon reconnoitred road for trench to W.Fs	
	but met a German party in Crater No 5. No	

Instructions regarding War Diaries and Intelligence Summaries are contained in F. S. Regs., Part II. and the Staff Manual respectively. Title pages will be prepared in manuscript.

WAR DIARY

or

INTELLIGENCE SUMMARY.

(Erase heading not required.)

Army Form C. 2118.

Hour, Date, Place	Summary of Events and Information	Remarks and References to Appendices
Dickebusch.		
	Connection could be made with W.F.s. 11 Others wounded.	
March 30th	Work as on 29th. Heavy shelling continued during night and pumping from Crater No 5.	
	1 Lieut Warner badly wounded in head.	
" 31st	Work as on 30th. One Cpl and one pioneer wounded. Two drivers accidentally wounded.	

(9 29 6) W 2794 100,000 8/14 H W V Forms/C. 2118/11.

3rd Divisional Engineers.

56TH FIELD COMPANY R.E.

APRIL 1 9 1 6.

56 F C R E 3

Vol. 19

Confidential

War Diary

of

56th Coy. R.E.

From April 1st to April 30th.
1916.

11/5/16.

[illegible] Capt R.E.

Instructions regarding War Diaries and Intelligence Summaries are contained in F. S. Regs., Part II. and the Staff Manual respectively. Title pages will be prepared in manuscript.

WAR DIARY
or
INTELLIGENCE SUMMARY.
(Erase heading not required.)

Army Form C. 2118.

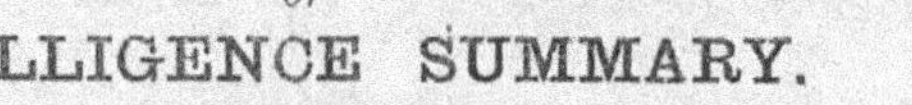

Hour, Date, Place	Summary of Events and Information	Remarks and References to Appendices
DICKEBUSCH.		
April 1st	Nos 2 & 3 Sections worked on bombing post leading out of T1. One loop hole revetted and block put in behind bombing post.	
	Nos 1 & 4 Sections worked on R3, repairing trench. CT behind trench repaired and three firing bays built up	
" 2nd	Nos 1 & 4 Sections could not join CT to crater No 4 as this was occupied by enemy, but worked on clearing R3 and R1. Nos 2 & 3 Sections were badly shelled in forward billets most of the dug outs being blown in. Sections scattered. about half were collected by 7 but were badly shaken and no work was done.	
" 8th	Attack on craters occupied by enemy. Nos 1, 2, 3 & 4 Sections worked on building up the new front line round the craters and improving the C.T. up to it (working strength small. Many men attending hospital).	

(9 29 6) W 2794 100,000 8/14 H W V Forms/C. 2118/11.

Instructions regarding War Diaries and Intelligence Summaries are contained in F. S. Regs., Part II. and the Staff Manual respectively. Title pages will be prepared in manuscript.

WAR DIARY
or
INTELLIGENCE SUMMARY.
(Erase heading not required.)

Army Form C. 2118.

Hour, Date, Place	Summary of Events and Information	Remarks and References to Appendices
DICKE BUSCH		
April 4th	Canadians took over line.	
	Nos 4 & 3 Sections went up to work but owing to a heavy bombardment and barrage were forced to return. Lieut Timmins(?) took a party up to inform O.C. Bench(?).	
5th	Coy packed	
6th	Coy moved back to rest billets at METEREN.	
METEREN 6–12th	Coy carried out usual 'rest' programme of drills etc.	
LA CLYTTE 13th	Coy moved to Billets at LA-CLYTTE.	
13th–19th	Coy worked on VIERSTRAAT switch. Night work.	
METEREN 19th–20th	Coy carried out usual 'rest' programme of drills etc.	
April 20th	Captain H. Pyne(?) took over the Company from Lieut A.W. Gordon.	
R.E. FARM ~~LA CLYTTE~~ 26th	The Coy moved to billets at R.E. FARM, LACLYTTE.	

(9 29 6) W 2794 100,000 8/14 H W V Forms/C. 2118/11.

Army Form C. 2118.

Instructions regarding War Diaries and Intelligence Summaries are contained in F. S. Regs., Part II. and the Staff Manual respectively. Title pages will be prepared in manuscript.

WAR DIARY
or
INTELLIGENCE SUMMARY.
(Erase heading not required.)

Hour, Date, Place	Summary of Events and Information	Remarks and References to Appendices
N15.c.2.3. R.E. FARM		
April 25th	No 1 Sectn worked on gap T2 - T3. Alarm for gas attack about 4.30. Sections withdrawn. No 2 Sectn worked on gap L1 - K2b.	
April 26 - 30th	Work on linking up gaps in front line trenches.	WS

W. Syme Capt RE.
O.C. 56th Coy. R.E.

(9 29 6) W 2794 100,000 8/14 H W V Forms/C. 2118/11.

3rd Divisional Engineers.

56TH FIELD COMPANY R.E.

MAY 1 9 1 6.

Instructions regarding War Diaries and Intelligence Summaries are contained in F. S. Regs., Part II. and the Staff Manual respectively. Title pages will be prepared in manuscript.

WAR DIARY
~~or~~
~~INTELLIGENCE~~ SUMMARY.

(*Erase heading not required.*)

Army Form C. 2118.

56th Field Co R.E.

Vol 20

Hour, Date, Place	Summary of Events and Information	Remarks and References to Appendices
1916.		
R.E. Farm N.15.C.2.3 (Sheet 28) May 1st – 10th.	Work on Front line with 2 Sections, joining up 'grouse' butts in Front line to continuous trench. Work in Carpenters shops and trench tram way.	H.B.
R.E. Farm N15.C.2.3. Sheet 28. May 11th to 18th. May 18th – do –	– do –	
19th to 23rd May	4 sections in front line joining up "grouse" butts in front line at night	[illegible]
R.E. farm N15.C.2.3 (sheet 28) 24th May – 31st May. La CLYTTE N7C8.10	2 sections VIERSTRAAT switch (subsidiary line) night & day work revetting etc. 2 sections training. Casualties. May 3rd Spr Airlie killed. 7th May wounded (at duty) Spr Starchland A. 10th May Sapper Warner C. killed 16th L/Cpl Kellie wounded (at duty). 20th May Sappers Wright Emmett & Gething wounded. 21st May Sappers Osber Matthews Last & Smith all wounded. 22nd May Cpl Young & Sapper Scott killed.	[illegible]

(9 29 6) W 2794 100,000 8/14 H W V Forms/C. 2118/11.

3rd Divisional Engineers.

56TH FIELD COMPANY R.E.

JUNE 1916.

Instructions regarding War Diaries and Intelligence Summaries are contained in F. S. Regs., Part II. and the Staff Manual respectively. Title pages will be prepared in manuscript.

WAR DIARY
or
INTELLIGENCE SUMMARY.
(Erase heading not required.)

Army Form C. 2118.

56 7a Coy R.E. III Vol 21

56th Fd Coy R.E.

Hour, Date, Place	Summary of Events and Information	Remarks and References to Appendices
LA CLYTTE N7C 8.10 Sheet 10. 1st June to 7th June	3 Sections VIERSTRAAT switch (subsidiary line) revetting wiring reclaiming etc. 1 section training	
8th June – 16th June	2 Sections working on VIERSTRAAT switch as above 2 Sections working on reclaiming communication trench (CONVENT LANE.) near ST ELOI.	
17th June	Marched LA CLYTTE to THIEUSHOEK Sheet 27 Q 35	
18th June	Marched THIEUSHOEK to WAEMARS CAPPEL I. 26 d.11	
19th "	Marched WAEMARS CAPPEL to LEDERZEELE G 22 c.0.5	
20th "	Marched LEDERZEELE to POLINCOVE 27a NE D29d 8.8.	
20th June to 1st July POLINCOVE	Training for offensive warfare.	

(9 29 6) W 2794 100,000 8/14 H W V Forms/C. 2118/11.

56TH FIELD COMPANY R.E.

JULY 1916.

Instructions regarding War Diaries and Intelligence Summaries are contained in F. S. Regs., Part II. and the Staff Manual respectively. Title Pages will be prepared in manuscript.

WAR DIARY
or
INTELLIGENCE SUMMARY
(Erase heading not required.)

Army Form C. 2118.

56th Field Coy RE

Place	Date	Hour	Summary of Events and Information	Remarks and references to Appendices
CARNOY	16.7.16		Company continued placing BAZENTIN LE GRAND in a state of defence making MG emplacements + loopholing + strengthening building for a keep. Moderately shelled all day.	
— do —	17.7.16 18.7.16		— do — Fairly heavily shelled all day	
— do —	19.7.16		— do — but brought in early as Divisional front was changed. 1 Sapper wounded.	
— do —	20.7.16		2 Sections working on roads, ½ in Camp resting	
	21.7.16		All company working on road CARNOY to MONTAUBAN.	
— do —	22.7.16		As on 21st. 1 man evacuated shellshock.	
— do —	23.7.16		Work at LONGUEVAL at night making breastwork + joining up C.T. + wiring front line. Fairly heavily shelled but only 2 casualties wounded. 1 shell shock.	
— do —	24.7.16		Ordered to work LONGUEVAL. C.T. work impossible owing to German Counter attack + heavy barrage.	
— do —	25.7.16		Marched to SANDPITS near BRAY to rest	
SANDPITS near BRAY	26.7.16		Resting	
	27.7.16		Marched to VILLE SUR ANCRE	
VILLE SUR ANCRE	28 to 31/7/16		RESTing. Drill + replenishment of stores etc.	[signature] Capt. Comdg 56th Fd Coy RE 1/8/16.

2449 Wt. W14957/M90 750,000 1/16 J.B.C. & A. Forms/C.2118/12.

Instructions regarding War Diaries and Intelligence Summaries are contained in F. S. Regs., Part II. and the Staff Manual respectively. Title pages will be prepared in manuscript.

WAR DIARY
or
INTELLIGENCE SUMMARY.
(Erase heading not required.)

Army Form C. 2118.

Vol 22

58th Fd Coy RE

Hour, Date, Place	Summary of Events and Information	Remarks and References to Appendices
Night 1st-2nd July BLINCOVE	Entrained at AUDRUICQ & trained to DOULLENS ~~arrived~~ from there marched to REBEAUCOURT & billeted.	
July 3 REBEAUCOURT	marched with 9th Bde group to HAVERNAC & billeted	
July 4 BERTANGLES July 5 LAHOUSSIE	marched with 9th Bde group to BERTANGLES & ~~bivouaced~~ billeted LAHOUSSIE & bivouaced	
July 6 BRAY	Marched independently to BRAY. Spent night in BRAY at 80th Coy HQ	
July 7 CARNOY	Company marched to CARNOY with watercart limbers forage cart only took over 80th Coy Dugouts. Section on forward dumps.	
July 8 CARNOY	Mounted Section & ~~[illegible]~~ Transport remained in BRAY and brought up stores daily from BRAY DUMPS. Tool carts left permanently at CARNOY. 2 sections making forward dumps 2 sections dug out dressing stations in CATERPILLAR VALLEY MAJOR HENDERSON wounded and one sapper Lt COMINS acting O.C.	

Instructions regarding War Diaries and Intelligence Summaries are contained in F. S. Regs., Part II. and the Staff Manual respectively. Title pages will be prepared in manuscript.

WAR DIARY
or
INTELLIGENCE SUMMARY.
(*Erase heading not required.*)

Army Form C. 2118.

56th Field Coy. RE

Hour, Date, Place	Summary of Events and Information	Remarks and References to Appendices
9.7.16. CARNOY	Work as day before on forward dumps and trench bridges	
10.7.16 CARNOY	Work as day before.	
11.7.16. CARNOY	Day 2 sections on forward dumps & trench bridging	
	Night 1 section on Dressing Station in Caterpillar Valley	
12.7.16 CARNOY	Day 2 sections forward dumps & trench bridging	
	Night 1 section on machine gun emplacement MARLBRO WOOD	
13.7.16 CARNOY	1 Section trench bridging 1 section making notice boards & fixing	
	4 route posts 2 Sections rested (one of which marked out route	
	MONTAUBAN ALLEY to CATERPILLAR VALLEY	
	Nos 1 & 2 Sections moved to position of assembly for attack S of	
	CATERPILLAR VALLEY at 10 pm & spent night there	
14.7.16.	At 8 am 1 & 2 sections advanced, assisted infantry	
	to clear village of BAZENTIN-LE GRAND & repell counterattacks.	
	Then loopholed and fortified farm in the village	
	Relieved at 6 pm by 3 & 4 sections who continued	
	work. Casualties 1 killed 17 wounded (and Pay Sergt at CARNOY)	

(9 29 6) W 2794 100,000 8/14 H W V Forms/C. 2118/11.

Army Form C. 2118.

Instructions regarding War Diaries and Intelligence Summaries are contained in F. S. Regs., Part II. and the Staff Manual respectively. Title Pages will be prepared in manuscript.

WAR DIARY
or
INTELLIGENCE SUMMARY 56th Coy R.E.

(Erase heading not required.)

56th Fd. Coy RE.

Place	Date	Hour	Summary of Events and Information	Remarks and references to Appendices
			Attack on BAZENTIN LE GRAND & LONGUEVAL by 3rd Div.	
CARNOY	14.7.16		About 8 a.m. Nos 1 & 2 sections advanced from gully behind CATERPILLAR VALLEY with 2 platoons K.R.R. Orders were to fortify farm in BAZENTIN-LE-GRAND. The 2 platoons K.R.R. were detailed to bring up wiring materials. Only 1 platoon ever arrived at B. le G. Nos 1 & 2 sections arrived at the village about 8.45 a.m. It had not been cleared of the enemy, & our infantry were on road S of village. Nos 1 & 2 sections & some 10th Liverpools cleared the village of enemy bombers & snipers who retired to a hollow on right flank 100 yards away & some machine guns were captured. Lt GORDON and 3 sappers brought in one machine gun. Nos 1 & 2 sections prepared & manned loopholes in keep (a very strong house in village) & 2 machine guns were emplaced. Fire from the keep & 2 stokes guns which came up drove off the Germans on our right flank & prevented reinforcements reaching them. They eventually retired. The machine guns then drove off a big counterattack on our left flank. The infantry then advanced to a line in front of village. The Germans then initiated a big frontal counterattack coming over ridge about 800x in front. Fire from the keep and artillery fire made them retire back over ridge. After this the village was shelled by the Germans; some of our heavy shells also fell short. The RE & KRR platoon then made barricades as shelling permitted outside the keep. At 6 pm Nos 1 & 2 sections were relieved by 3 & 4 sections. The farm was heavily shelled, damage being done to front walls & cellars. Upper story which had been manned & loopholed in the morning was destroyed. Casualties 1 killed 16 wounded and Pay Sergt at CARNOY killed (6 wounded 1 & 2 sections, 1 killed 10 wounded 3 & 4 sections)	
CARNOY	15.7.16.		Whole company continued work of fortifying keep. MAJOR HENDERSON returned to duty. A well was put in working order, machine gun emplacements begun at BAZENTIN LE GRAND, NS road through village cleared. Casualties 1 wounded.	

2449 Wt. W14957/M90 750,000 1/16 J.B.C. & A. Forms/C.2118/12.

3rd Divisional Engineers

56th FIELD COMPANY R. E.

AUGUST 1 9 1 6

Army Form C. 2118.

WAR DIARY
or
INTELLIGENCE SUMMARY
(Erase heading not required.)

Instructions regarding War Diaries and Intelligence Summaries are contained in F. S. Regs., Part II. and the Staff Manual respectively. Title Pages will be prepared in manuscript.

56th Field Coy RE

Vol 23

Place	Date	Hour	Summary of Events and Information	Remarks and references to Appendices
VILLE sous CORBIE	August 1st to 10th		Training [illegible] rest area - drills etc	
SANDPITS	11th		Marched to SANDPITS & bivouacked	
Sheet 57 D(SE) E 18 d 4.0. SANDPITS	12 & 13th		Resting & 1 Section practising strong points	
CITADEL Sheet 57 D SE F 15 c 9.3.	14th		Marched to CITADEL continuous work night & day with all sections on dugouts for Brigade Headquarters CHIMPANZEE TRENCH	
MINDEN POST near CARNOY.	15th		— do — but marched to MINDEN POST near CARNOY	
	16		— do — also NO 2 Section attached to 9th Bde for work but attack unsuccessful no work was done. Spr Wright wounded since deceased	
	17th		No 2 Section with 9th Bde 2 Lieut SMITH + 5 NCOs laid out tape for attack on Lonely Trench in front of existing front line 9 p.m. L/Cpl Webster wounded.	
	18th		No 1 Section attached to 9th Brigade but owing to unsuccessful attack were not used.	
	19th		All Company worked by day improving Jackson C.T. Lieut WILLIAMSON and 2 men with [illegible] working party dug C.T by night to LONELY-TRENCH was abandoned by Enemy	
CITADEL	20th		Marched to CITADEL bivouacked.	

2449 Wt. W14957/M90 750,000 1/16 J.B.C. & A. Forms/C.2118/12.

2 Army Form C. 2118.

WAR DIARY
or
INTELLIGENCE SUMMARY
(Erase heading not required.)

Instructions regarding War Diaries and Intelligence Summaries are contained in F. S. Regs., Part II. and the Staff Manual respectively. Title Pages will be prepared in manuscript.

56th Fd Coy RE

Place	Date August	Hour	Summary of Events and Information	Remarks and references to Appendices
VILLE sur ANCRE	21st		Marched to VILLE sur ANCRE.	
— do —	22nd		Dismounted portion VILLE. Transport to LANCHES in 2 days march	
LANCHES	23rd		Dismounted portion entrained at MARICOURT for LANCHES	
— do —	24th		At LANCHES.	
MÉZEROLLES	25th		Marched to MÉZEROLLES	
NEUVILLE au CORNET	26th		Marched to NEUVILLE au CORNET	
PETIT ANVIN	27th		Marched to PETIT ANVIN.	
— do —	28th		At PETIT ANVIN. Drilled	
TANGRY	29th		Marched to TANGRY	
MARLES ~~MAZINGARBE~~ LES MINES	30th		Marched to ~~MAZINGARBE~~ MARLES LES MINES	
~~[illegible]~~	~~31st~~		~~[illegible] VILLE ST. ARNOULD~~ [illegible]	
MAZINGARBE	31st		Marched to MAZINGARBE	

[signature] Major
Comdg 56th Fd Coy RE

56TH FIELD COMPANY R.E.

SEPTEMBER 1 9 1 6.

Instructions regarding War Diaries and Intelligence Summaries are contained in F. S. Regs., Part II. and the Staff Manual respectively. Title Pages will be prepared in manuscript.

WAR DIARY
or
~~INTELLIGENCE~~ SUMMARY
(Erase heading not required.)

SEPTEMBER 1916.

56th Fd Co RE

Army Form C. 2118.

VM 24

Place	Date	Hour	Summary of Events and Information	Remarks and references to Appendices
MAZINGARBE	1st 2nd		Work on sanitation and improvements to billets	
	3rd 4th		1 section making forward billets. remr work on camp improvements.	
	5th to 11th		All sections at work continuously on mined dugouts in Reserve trench. 6 hours actual work on face.	
	12th		2 fresh dugouts started in POSEN & RAILWAY alleys.	
	12th to 20th		All sections continuously at work on mined dugouts as above	
AUCHEL	21st		Coy marched to AUCHEL	
	22nd		Marched to CUHEM.	
CUHEM	23rd to 30th		Training at CUHEM for offensive operations.	

[illegible] Major
Comdg 56th Fd Co R.E.

2449 Wt. W14957/M90 750,000 1/16 J.B.C. & A. Forms/C.2118/12.

3rd Divisional Engineers.

56TH FIELD COMPANY R.E.

OCTOBER 1 9 1 6.

Instructions regarding War Diaries and Intelligence Summaries are contained in F. S. Regs., Part II. and the Staff Manual respectively. Title Pages will be prepared in manuscript.

WAR DIARY or INTELLIGENCE SUMMARY

(Erase heading not required.)

Original

56th Fd Coy. RE.

Vol 24

Place	Date	Hour	Summary of Events and Information	Remarks and references to Appendices
CUHEM.	1st to 4th		Training & manoeuvres.	
HERNICOURT.	5th		Marched to HERNICOURT with 9th Bde.	
HERNICOURT	6th 7th		Dismounted in HERNICOURT mounted portion by road to CANNEMONT.	
— do — On Rail	7th 8th		Dismounted by rail & march route to BEAUSSART arrived 11 pm. 8th. (ACHEUX inserted above)	
BEAUSSART.	9th to 12th		2 sections mined dugouts for Divisional & Bde Hd Qrs Southern Avenue. 2 sections dugouts for bomb stores. Continuous shifts. Carpenters running dump, shops etc.	
BEAUSSART	13th.		all company mined dugouts Divisional & Bde Hd Qrs. & running shops for carpenters work such as duckboards trench bridges etc etc. Made prisoners cage.	
BEAUSSART	13th to 18th		All company continuous work mined dugouts & running dump shops as above.	
COURCELLES	19th		Marched to COURCELLES work as for 13th to 18th.	
COURCELLES	20th to 28th		Continuous work mined dugouts Divisional & Bde H. Qrs. running dump at COURCELLES making trench bridges, duckboards, torpedoes etc etc.	
COURCELLES	28th to 31st.		As above also connecting up new tramway EUSTON to SUCRERIE. Dugouts Completed 30th & men resting 31st.	

[illegible signature] Commd 56th Fd Coy RE.

2449 Wt. W14957/M90 750,000 1/16 J.B.C. & A. Forms/C.2118/12.

File

①

9th Bde.

Herewith sketch & suggested organization for a 2 strong point.

It is of course not complete as regards small points of organization which must be thought out in each case.

I will send a suggested drill later for six men to do the work shown in the sketch.

M. [illegible]

[illegible]

6/10/16 Comd 51st [illegible]

[illegible]

---

②

Suggested Z strong point for 10 to 15 men + 2 M.G.'s.

① Design is shewn on attached sketch.

② 3 Tapes are made up beforehand as follows. 15' 6' 15' 6' 15'

A A.

The lot A A being connected by a bit of string. The strong point can then be laid out in 2 minutes. 1 peg each end.

③ The endeavour has been to provide all round fire & an obstacle quickly & then to deepen the trench & complete the obstacle subsequently.

④ Given a working party of 50 Inf. + 3 Sappers the work might be somewhat as follows.

1-

(3)

1st night

Organization. (2 shovels + 1 pick to 3 men told off to dig).

Carrying

20 men French wire + 1 shovel or pick
13 men 2 pickets 1 shovel or pick
8 men 1 coil of barbed wire + staples.
9 men 4 pickets
3 sappers. 3 shovels 1 tape 1 picket
6 prs of hedging gloves + 3 wire cutters to be taken too

Jobs. Sappers. Front M G Emplacement

33 men digging

17 wiring & providing casualties in 2 parties of 6 (5 men spare)

They should be able to dig out the 1st shelf & possibly the recesses & put out an obstacle of French wire picketed every 3 yards with 3 strands of barbed wire thro' it

(4)

2nd night.

Very much as for 1st night except that tools will not require to be carried.
Complete trench & 2nd row of French wire. Arrange for storage places for water bombs. ammun etc.

3rd night.

Complete obstacle as in sketch dig ~~out~~ shelter for M.G. crew + for others where possible
To complete obstacle as per sketch without loose filling in coils requires 30 coils of wire + 140 odd small pickets.

N.B. mauls will be required if screw pickets are not available

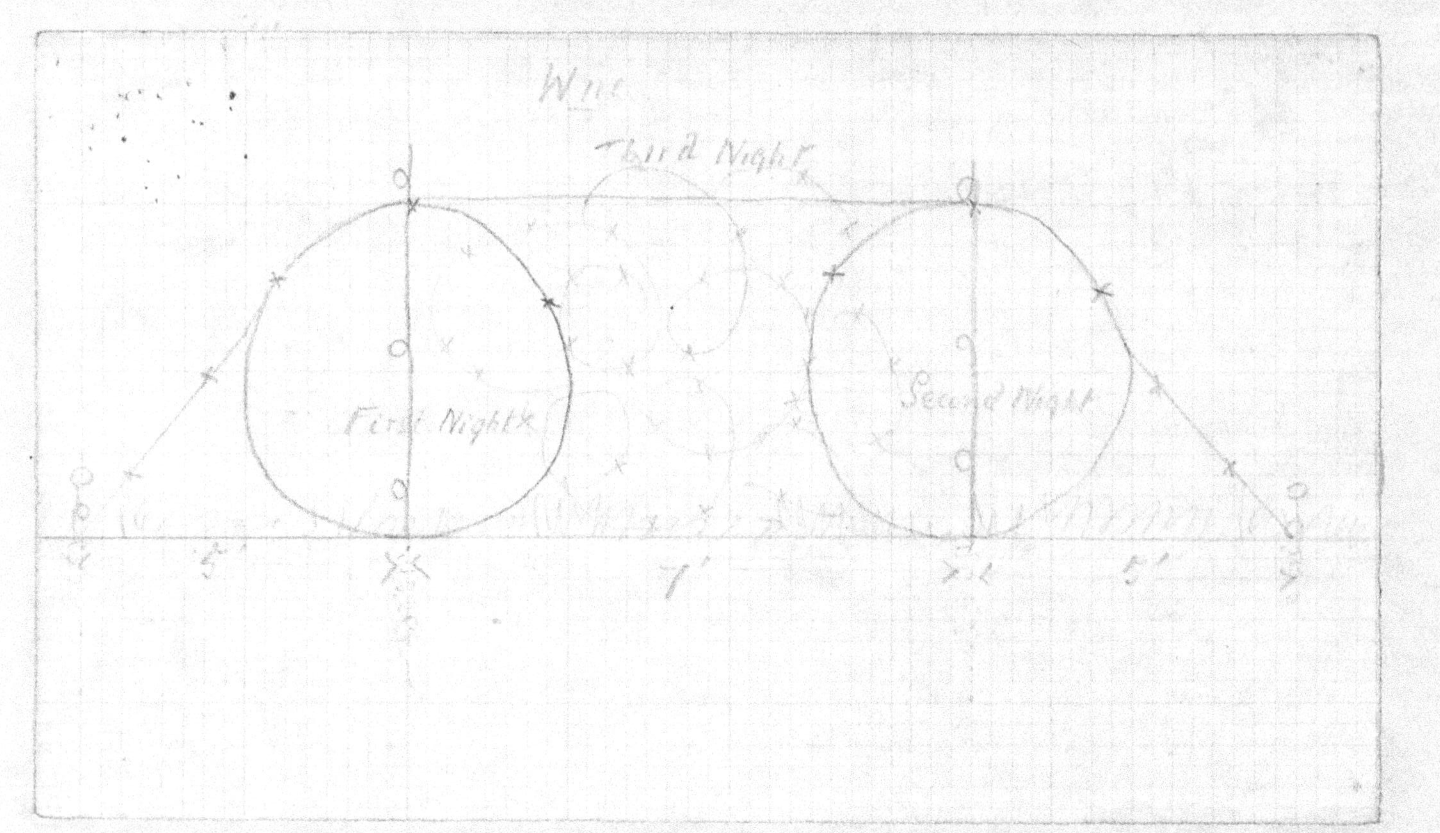
Wire
Third Night
First Night
Second Night
5'
7'
5'

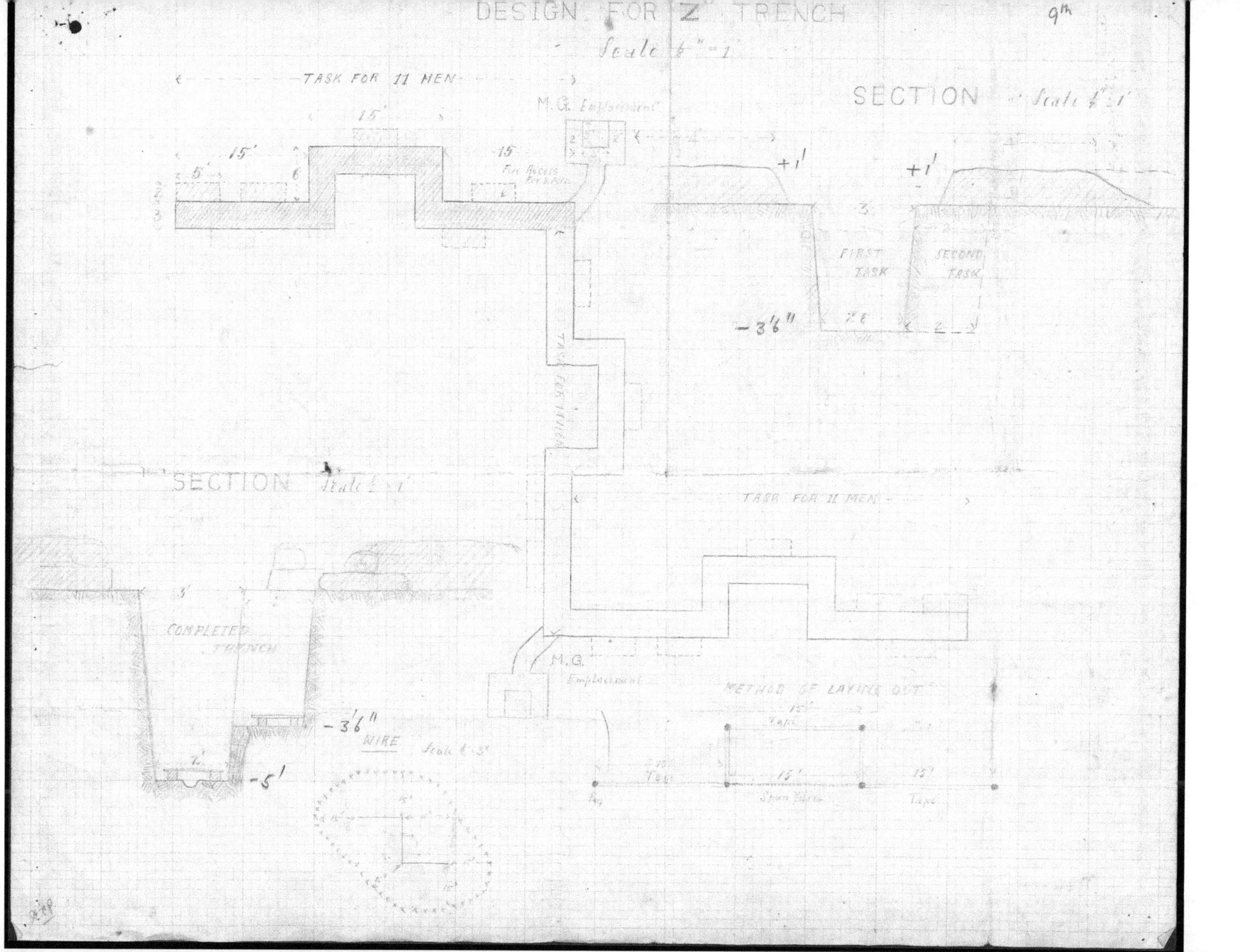
DESIGN FOR Z TRENCH
9th
TASK FOR 11 MEN
M.G. Emplacement
SECTION
COMPLETED TRENCH
FIRST TASK
SECOND TASK
TASK FOR 11 MEN
M.G. Emplacement
METHOD OF LAYING OUT
WIRE
-3'6"
-5'
+1'

MAP OF SERRE Scale 1/2500
A
B
C
D
E
F
K30

56TH FIELD COMPANY R.E.

NOVEMBER 1 9 1 6.

Army Form C. 2118.

Instructions regarding War Diaries and Intelligence Summaries are contained in F. S. Regs., Part II. and the Staff Manual respectively. Title Pages will be prepared in manuscript.

WAR DIARY
or
INTELLIGENCE SUMMARY
(Erase heading not required.)

56th Fd Coy RE

Vol 26

Place	Date	Hour	Summary of Events and Information	Remarks and references to Appendices
COURCELLES	1st		Resting in billets	
"	2nd to [illegible]		3 sections work Trench mortar emplacements near front line ~~[illegible]~~ remdr working in dump trench bridges ladders etc. Parties at work on roads light railway todds [illegible]	
"	11th		2 sections work on bomb stores near Euston & Northern Avenue	
"	12th		Remr working on dump.	
	13th		In reserve Offensive operations	
"	14th		~~[illegible]~~ All sections clearing dugouts blown in Rob Roy, Monk & Taupin	
"	15th		2 sections T M Emplacements 10 men on Bomb Stores remainder R E Yard	
"	16th		2 sections T M Emplacements 2 sections R E Dump.	
	17th		Ditto	
	18th		Ditto and 6 men & 50 inf on COURCELLES – COLINCAMPS road	
	19th		Ditto	
	20th		Ditto	
	21st		Ditto	
	22nd		Ditto	

[illegible] RE

2449 Wt. W14957/M90 750,000 1/16 J.B.C. & A. Forms/C.2118/12.

Instructions regarding War Diaries and Intelligence Summaries are contained in F. S. Regs., Part II. and the Staff Manual respectively. Title Pages will be prepared in manuscript.

Army Form C. 2118.

WAR DIARY
or
INTELLIGENCE SUMMARY
(Erase heading not required.)

56 Field Company RE

Place	Date	Hour	Summary of Events and Information	Remarks and references to Appendices
COURCELLES	23.11		1 section T.M. Emplacement Road parties on COURCELLES – COLINCAMPS road day COLINCAMPS EUSTON road night 2 sections bus road parties on RE Dump. 1 section on reclaiming WICKER TRENCH	
	24-11		—— Ditto ——	
	25.11		—— Ditto ——	
	26 11		—— Ditto ——	
	27 11		1½ sections WICKER TRENCH ½ section RE Yard & Road Parties 2 sections resting	
	28.11		2 sections on WICKER TRENCH 2 sections less 6 men RE Yard Road Parties 6 RE + 50 Inf.	
	29 11		—— Ditto —— and trace 10 infan OP at CRA dugout	
	30.11		—— ditto ——	[illegible]

2449 Wt. W14957/M90 750,000 1/16 J.B.C. & A. Forms/C.2118/12.

CRE III Division

The following casualties were omitted from the original copy of War diary of this Company for the Month of Nov 1916. Will you kindly pass this on so that they may be inserted at the end of the diary. The duplicate copy has this inserted.

41145	Driver Sharpe W.	} Killed in action 13/11/16	
20268	" Crockford C	}	
20559	" Ward. J S.	Died of wounds received in action 13/11/16	
33236	" Penman. G.	}	
12585	" Bye. G.	}	
12590	" Garrard. P.	} Wounded 13/11/16	
17174	" Cox. H T.	}	
12592	" Smith. T.	}	
28300	a/Lce Cpl Bastable. G.H	Killed in Action 15/11/16	
	II Lieut D. L. Savage.	Died of Wounds received in action 15/11/16	
31017	Sapper. Gill. L.	Accidentally wounded 22/11/16	

Error regretted.

26 12/16

[signature] Major RE
OC 56th Field Co RE

3rd Divisional Engineers.

56TH FIELD COMPANY R.E.

DECEMBER 1 9 1 6.

3

A.A. & Q.M.G.
a
7815/a/25
3RD DIVISION

Officer i/c Adjutant General's
Office at the Base.

Will you please make the necessary insertions.

A.G.'s OFFICE AT THE BASE
CENTRAL REGISTRY
28 DEC 1916
C. R. No. ____

A.G.'s OFFICE AT THE BASE
SORTING OFFICE
28 DEC 1916
27/12/16.
C. R.

[signature]
Major-General,
Commanding 3rd Division.

56 Fd Coy RE
App C Vol 26

CRE III Division

Herewith original Copy of War Diary of this Company for the Month of Decr. 1916

[signature] Major RE

1/1/17

OC 56th Field Co RE

Instructions regarding War Diaries and Intelligence Summaries are contained in F. S. Regs., Part II. and the Staff Manual respectively. Title Pages will be prepared in manuscript.

WAR DIARY
or
INTELLIGENCE SUMMARY

(Erase heading not required.)

Army Form C. 2118.

Vol 27

56th Co 4 RE

Place	Date	Hour	Summary of Events and Information	Remarks and references to Appendices
COURCELLES.	1st to 22nd inst.		2 sections at work by night with Infy parties reclaiming WICKER TRENCH + improving dug out accommodation 2 sections by day at work in R.E. Yard making U. Frames duck walks, frames for dugouts, painting boards etc. etc. 3 men with Infy party on road COURCELLES. – EUSTON DUMP. odd men Gut to different regts etc. Constructing O.P.'s T.M. emplacements etc. 1 day per fortnight holiday except for Clean arms gas helmet etc inspection.	
COURCELLES	23rd 24th inst.		2 sections + odd jobs as above 1 section WICKER TRENCH as above 1 section reclaiming 6th Avenue by day	
COURCELLES.	25th		Xmas. day. no work.	
COURCELLES	26th to 29th		Work as on 23rd + 24th.	
COURCELLES	30th 31st		2 sections R.E. Yard as from 1st to 22nd + odd jobs as above 2 sections reclaiming 6th Avenue 1 day 1 night Wounded 31st inst. No 134949 Sapper G. Pascoe	

[illegible signature]
Commd 56th [illegible]

2449 Wt. W14957/M90 750,000 1/16 J.B.C. & A. Forms/C.2118/12.

3rd Division

War Diary

56th F. Coy.

January to December

1917

Army Form C. 2118.

Vol 28

56th Fd Coy RE.

Instructions regarding War Diaries and Intelligence Summaries are contained in F. S. Regs., Part II. and the Staff Manual respectively. Title Pages will be prepared in manuscript.

WAR DIARY
or
INTELLIGENCE SUMMARY

(Erase heading not required.)

Place	Date	Hour	Summary of Events and Information	Remarks and references to Appendices
COURCELLES.	1st to 8th.		2 sections 1 day 1 night reclaiming 6th Avenue (C.T.) 2 sections working in RE Yard by day making duckwalks V. Frames. dugout frames etc etc. Infantry attached mining & carrying. Lieut. Cummins wounded 4. 1. 17.	
BEAUSSART	9th.		Marched to BEAUSSART.	
BEAUSSART	10th.		All sections working on YELLOW LINE near BEAUMONT HAMEL by day. wiring. dugouts. M.G. emplacements etc.	
— do —	11th.		Improvements to billets in camp no work on line owing to attack.	
— do —	12th to 16th		All sections work as on Tenth inst.	
— do —	17th		Holiday & cleaning up. Driving snow prevented work.	

2449 Wt. W14957/M90 750,000 1/16 J.B.C. & A. Forms/C.2118/12.

Army Form C. 2118.

Instructions regarding War Diaries and Intelligence Summaries are contained in F. S. Regs., Part II. and the Staff Manual respectively. Title Pages will be prepared in manuscript.

WAR DIARY
or
INTELLIGENCE SUMMARY
(Erase heading not required.)

Place	Date	Hour	Summary of Events and Information	Remarks and references to Appendices
BEAUSSART	18th		All sections worked on YELLOW LINE.	
"	24th		One sapper wounded on 24th.	
"	25th		Gas helmet drill. One officer wounded. Capt Ernst RAMC (att'd)	
"	26th		Coy worked on yellow line	
"	27th		Coy worked on yellow line	
SARTON.	28th		Marched to SARTON.	
REBREUVE	29th		Marched to REBREUVE	
"	30th		Marched to GUINECOURT.	
"	31st		Marched to BIEVAL.	

A W Gordon HRE.
for O. C. 56 Coy RE

2449 Wt. W14957/M90 750,000 1/16 J.B.C. & A. Forms/C.2118/12.

Instructions regarding War Diaries and Intelligence Summaries are contained in F. S. Regs., Part II. and the Staff Manual respectively. Title Pages will be prepared in manuscript.

WAR DIARY
or
INTELLIGENCE SUMMARY
(Erase heading not required.)

Army Form C. 2118.

~~8~~ 56 3rd Coy R.E.

Vol 29

Place	Date	Hour	Summary of Events and Information	Remarks and references to Appendices
DIEVAL	2.2.17	-	Two Sections consisting of ~~70~~ Two Officers and 70 O.R. dispatched to HCQ for work there under C.R.E. Putting up Nissen Huts, they erected in all 15 Huts. HJ	
	2.2.17	to 8.2.17	Coy at Rest. HJ	
	8.2.17		Marched to. HJ	
	8.2.17	11.2.17	Coy at Rest. HJ	
	11.2.17	-	Marched to ARRAS. Took up Billets in RUE ST. CLAIRE. HJ	
	12.2.17	-	Took over Front line RE Work. HJ	
	13.2.17	-	Started night work on Divisional Front, putting in new Traverses. HJ	
	16.2.17	-	No 2 3 4 Sect. Started work on 9th Bde H.Qs. HJ	
	17.2.17	-	No 2 Sect. started work on 2 Batt. H.Qs. HJ	
	18.2.17	-	Work continued of Traverse and dugouts, two men wounded in Front line. HJ	by
	19.2.17	-	One N.C.O. and 3 Sappers commence work in strengthening ~~dugout~~ Tunnel across Cambrai Road in Front line, a very warm corner. HJ	
	22.2.17		Finished work on Tunnel in Front line under Cambrai Arras Road. HJ	
	23.2.17		Continued work on Bde & Batt dugouts off KING STREET TUNNEL. HJ	
	24.2.17		—Do— —Do—	
	25.2.17		Started on completing Road across Railway lines at Arras Station. HJ	
	26.2.17		—Do— —Do—	
	27.2.17		The 76th Bde went to rest and 8th Bde came into line. HJ	
	28.2.17		Started on T.M. Battery dugouts. HJ	

H.W. Forth Major
O.C. 56th Fld Coy R.E.

2449 Wt. W14957/M90 750,000 1/16 J.B.C. & A. Forms/C.2118/12.

Army Form C. 2118.

Instructions regarding War Diaries and Intelligence Summaries are contained in F. S. Regs., Part II. and the Staff Manual respectively. Title Pages will be prepared in manuscript.

WAR DIARY
or
INTELLIGENCE SUMMARY
(Erase heading not required.)

Vol 30

Place	Date	Hour	Summary of Events and Information	Remarks and references to Appendices
ARRAS	1st	–	Worked on Bde – Batty Dugouts 3 T. M Dugouts and boot cover, Arras St. H.F.	H.F.
"	2nd	–	No 2 Section helped to dig men out of trench that had fallen in. H.F.	
"	3rd	–	Work as usual. H.F.	
"	4th	–	Work as usual. H.F.	
"	5th	–	Successful Raid by 1st Gordons & Sappers of company blew up two dugouts with out casualties to Sappers. H.F.	
"	6th	–	The Battalion Dugout complete. H.F.	
	7th	-	Work as usual H.F.	
	8th	-	Bde H.Q. completed. H.F.	
	9th	-	Started on "A" T.M. Battery near Island Street. H.F.	
	10th	-	Cleaning out tunnel near Bde H.Q. H.F.	
	11th	-	Work as usual H.F.	
	12th	-	Lt. Williamson was killed at 10.15 pm. working on support lines near Imperial	
	13th		× 2 Cpl. Johnson } Street, two other men wounded. Started "B" T.M. Battery. H.F.	
			Started work on strengthening tunnel to Bde H.Q. H.F. Capt Gordon went to instruct	
	14th	-	Officers at Div School. Recommenced work on support line. H.F.	
	15th		Work as usual. H.F.	
	16th		Sap. Forsyth was given Military Medal for good work in the Raid. H.F.	

2449 Wt. W14957/M90 750,000 1/16 J.B.C. & A. Forms/C.2118/12.

Army Form C. 2118.

Instructions regarding War Diaries and Intelligence Summaries are contained in F. S. Regs., Part II. and the Staff Manual respectively. Title Pages will be prepared in manuscript.

WAR DIARY
or
INTELLIGENCE SUMMARY

(Erase heading not required.)

Place	Date	Hour	Summary of Events and Information	Remarks and references to Appendices
ARRAS.	17.	–	Trench mortars proceeding. H.J.	
	18.	–	Work as usual. H.J.	
	19.	–		
	20.	–	Germans commenced retiring from half of our front we started C.T across no mans land. H.J.	
	21	–	Completed C.T across no mans land. H.J.	
	22	–	Started work on Div H.Q. in Russel Caves. H.J.	
	23	–	Work as usual. H.J.	
	24	–	Commenced clearing bag out in Bosh lines. H.J.	
	25	–	Work as usual. H.J.	
	26	–	Completed. Divisional H.Q. H. H.J.	
	27	–	Clearing up our Cellar Billets. H.J.	
	28	–	Commenced O.P. in Bosh lines. H.J.	
	29	–	Completed Bosh dugout traverses. H.J.	
	30	–	Had a practice of digging Strong Points for offensive. H.J.	
	31st	–	Started moving into cellar Billets, in ARRAS. H.J.	
	5th		No 32966 a/Lce Cpl Thompson wounded "at duty"	
	17th		No 145609 Sapper Shaw J. " "	
			" 67191 " Palmer J. wounded	
	21st		" 56072 " Bridges. A "	
	"		" 43195 " Whitehurst J "	

HWD Trot. Major.
O.C. 56th Fld Coy RE.
31-3-17.

2449 Wt. W14957/M90 750,000 1/16 J.B.C. & A. Forms/C.2118/12.

Instructions regarding War Diaries and Intelligence Summaries are contained in F. S. Regs., Part II. and the Staff Manual respectively. Title Pages will be prepared in manuscript.

WAR DIARY
or
INTELLIGENCE SUMMARY

(Erase heading not required.)

Army Form C. 2118.

Original 3rd

56th 1st QRE April 1917

Vol 31

Place	Date	Hour	Summary of Events and Information	Remarks and references to Appendices
ARRAS.	1-4-17 to 2-4-17		Coy working on improving new Billets in ARRAS. H.Y.	
	3-4-17		Making O.P. in front of TILLOY VILLAGE. H.Y.	
	4-4-17		Making Screen on CAMBRIA ROAD. H.Y.	
	9-4-17		No 1.2.3 Section went forward after the storming party and consolidated TILLOY.	
			No 4. inspected Boche Dugouts and got wells into working order H.Y.	
			The following were our casualties: Lt Crane wounded. No 44725 Pioneer Crellin H ×	
			No 33053 Sap. Fowler T. wounded. H.Y.	
	10-4-17		Repairing roads into TILLOY H.Y.	
	11-4-17		— do —	
	12-4-17		— do —	
	13-4-17		No 1.2 Sections moved forward to TILLOY to support 9th Bde in taking GUEMAPPE H.Y.	
	14-4-17		Division went into Rest. H.Y.	
	15-4-17 to 21-4-17		Coy at Rest. H.Y.	
	22-4-17			
	23-4-17		Made Advance H.Q. at to the North of TILLOY. H.Y.	
	24-4-17		— do — — do —	
	25-4-17		Commenced repairing Dugouts for III Div H.Q. EAST of TILLOY.	
			No 23661 L/Sergt Jenkins H wounded on CAMBRIA ROAD by shell — since died H.Y.	
	26-4-17		Repairing Div H.Q. H.Y. 2nd Lt. Foxon joined the Coy from draft. H.Y.	
	27-4-17		— do —	
	28-4-17		Repairing fair weather road to the north of TILLOY. H.Y.	
	29-4-17		2nd Lt. Waddilove joined the Coy H.Y.	
	30-4-17		Repairing fair weather road to the North of TILLOY. H.Y.	H.W. Ford Major.

2449 Wt. W14957/M90 750,000 1/16 J.B.C. & A. Forms/C.2118/12.

Army Form C. 2118.

Instructions regarding War Diaries and Intelligence Summaries are contained in F. S. Regs., Part II. and the Staff Manual respectively. Title Pages will be prepared in manuscript.

WAR DIARY
or
INTELLIGENCE SUMMARY

(Erase heading not required.)

56th Field CoRE

Place	Date	Hour	Summary of Events and Information	Remarks and references to Appendices
TILLOY	1/5/17		Nos 2 3 + 4 sections repairing fair weather track to the north of TILLOY.	
			No 1 Section making barbed wire aprons.	
— " —	2/5/17		Nos 1 2 3 + 4 sections repairing fair weather track — " —	
— " —	3/5/17		Standing by for orders to consolidate new line.	
— " —	4/5/17		Nos 1 2 3 + 4 sections wiring front line in front of MONCHY-LE-PREUX.	
— " —	5/5/17		— " — — " — Wiring	
— " —	6/5/17		— " — — " — — " — — " — Nos [illegible] Sapper [illegible] wounded [illegible] (O.P. [illegible] MONCHY)	
— " —	7/5/17		— " — — " — — " —	
— " —	8/5/17		— " — — " — — " —	
— " —	9/5/17		— " — — " — — " — — " — No [illegible] Sapper [illegible] wounded [illegible] MONCHY No [illegible] [illegible] [illegible] [illegible]	
— " —	10/5/17		No 1 section Wiring	
			No 2 section draining trench (Nos 3 + 4 sections resting)	
— " —	11/5/17		No 4 Section Constructing aid post. (Nos 1 2 + 3 sections standing by)	
— " —	12/5/17		No 4 — " — Nos 1 2 + 3 Sections wiring	
— " —	13/5/17		No 4 — " — Completed Aid post	
— " —	— " —		No 3 — " — Wiring	
— " —	14/5/17		Handed over to F.C. Co of 29th Div and marched to SIMENCOURT at night	
SIMENCOURT	15/5/17		[illegible]	
— " —	16/5/17		Inspection of billets, arms, + accoutrements.	

2449 Wt. W14957/M90 750,000 1/16 J.B.C. & A. Forms/C.2118/12.

Instructions regarding War Diaries and Intelligence Summaries are contained in F. S. Regs., Part II. and the Staff Manual respectively. Title Pages will be prepared in manuscript.

WAR DIARY
or
INTELLIGENCE SUMMARY

(Erase heading not required.)

Army Form C. 2118.

Place	Date	Hour	Summary of Events and Information	Remarks and references to Appendices
SIMENCOURT	17/5/17		(wet weather no parades)	
— " —	18/5/17		Marched to LIENCOURT	
LIENCOURT	19/5/17		Mounted, marched to St POL (XVIII Corps Depot Camp)	
— " —	[illegible]		Dismounted, proceeded by [illegible]	
St POL	[illegible]		Church parade 9.15 AM.	
— " —	[illegible]		Physical exercises & squad drill (1 NCO & 12 sappers proceeded to [illegible]VILLE Camp for work.)	
	[illegible]		Nos 1 & 2 Sections employed in XVIII Corps Depot camp.	
	[illegible]		Nos 3 & 4 — " — Physical exercises & squad drill. All NCOs except [illegible] communicating drill.	
	[illegible]		— Do — — Do —	
	[illegible]		Nos 3 & 4 sections employed in XVIII Corps Depot Camp. — Do —	
	[illegible]		Nos 1 & 2 — " — Physical exercises & squad drill. Party of 10 men cleaning up Coy [illegible]	
	[illegible]		— Do — — Do —	
	[illegible]		— Do — — Do — [illegible] joined from [illegible]	
	[illegible]		Whole company paraded for baths (Sunday) 1 NCO & 12 sappers rejoined from [illegible]VILLE CAMP.	
	[illegible]		Nos 3 & 4 sections drill. Nos 1 & 2 sections work in Depot Camp. NCOs communicating drill and NCOs & men [illegible]	
	[illegible]		Nos 1, 2, 3 & 4 sections (less [illegible] men inoculated) work in Depot Camp. NCOs communicating drill	
— " —	[illegible]		All sections Physical exercises, squad drill & company drill	
	[illegible]		— Do —	

[illegible]

Major RE
[illegible] 56th [illegible] Co RE

2449 Wt. W14957/M90 750,000 1/16 J.B.C. & A. Forms/C.2118/12.

Instructions regarding War Diaries and Intelligence Summaries are contained in F. S. Regs., Part II. and the Staff Manual respectively. Title Pages will be prepared in manuscript.

WAR DIARY
or
~~INTELLIGENCE SUMMARY~~

(Erase heading not required.)

Army Form C. 2118.

56th Field Co RE

Vol 33

Place	Date	Hour	Summary of Events and Information	Remarks and references to Appendices
ST. POL	1/6/17		Packing up for move to ARRAS.	
— " —	2/6/17		Dismounted portion of company proceeded by busses to ARRAS & from ARRAS to Camp near FEUCHY by rail. Mounted portion proceeded by road to ARRAS.	
Camp near FEUCHY	3/6/17		Church Parade 9.30 A.M. (dismounted). Mounted section proceeded by road to ARRAS.	
	4/6/17		No. 1, 3 & 4 sections worked on mined Dugouts from 8.0 AM – 5.0 A.M. in reliefs.	
— " —	5/6/17		Whole company work on dugouts.	
RAILWAY TRIANGLE	6/6/17		— " —	
— " —	7/6/17		3 sections working on Dugouts 1 section resting in billets	
— " —	8/6/17		Whole company working on Dugouts.	
— " —	9/6/17		2 sections working on Dugouts 1 section making new company billet 1 section resting	
— " —	10/6/17		2 sections working on new company billet 2 sections standing by for ...	
— " —	11/6/17		Whole company working on Dugouts	
	12/6/17		Dismounted portion of company moved to new billet N. of TILLOY	
			Whole company working on Dugouts.	
Dugouts N of TILLOY	15/6/17		Whole company working on Dugouts. No. 18913 Sapper Clews J. } " 480631 — " — Hawkes? H.H. } killed in action " 476528 — " — Hughes ... } " 424764 — " — Greenwood W. died of wounds received in action Major E. H. ... 2nd Lt. ... 33155 Sapper Ferris J. 24712 — " — Reynolds A. S. 352679 — " — Ward C. 136693 — " — Goddard W. R. 139143 — " — Cliff F. C. No. 145055 Cpl. Quin? ... " 134046 " Barman? ... " 14512 " Swaingers? ...	wounded

2449 Wt. W14957/M90 750,000 1/16 J.B.C. & A. Forms/C.2118/12.

Instructions regarding War Diaries and Intelligence Summaries are contained in F. S. Regs., Part II. and the Staff Manual respectively. Title Pages will be prepared in manuscript.

WAR DIARY
or
INTELLIGENCE SUMMARY
(Erase heading not required.)

Army Form C. 2118.

56th Field CoRE

Place	Date	Hour	Summary of Events and Information	Remarks and references to Appendices
Dugouts N. of TILLOY	14/6/17		3 sections working on Dugouts	
— " —	15/6/17		Whole Company — " —	
— " —	16/6/17		Reliefs from all sections working on Dugouts	
— " —	17/6/17		— " — — " — No. 33973 Sapper Redman wounded (remained at duty)	
— " —	18/6/17		Company marched to ARRAS.	
ARRAS	19/6/17		Resting	
— " —	20/6/17		Company marched to GOUY-en-ARTOIS.	
GOUY-en-ARTOIS	21/6/17		Resting.	
— " —	22/6/17		Training.	
— " —	23/6/17 to 29/6/17		2 sections training. 2 sections building sheds etc for ammunition dump near WANQUETIN	
— " —	30/6/17		Company proceeded to ACHIET-LE-PETIT. Dismounted by Buses, Mounted by road.	

A W Brown Major R.E.
2/7/17 O.C. 56th Fd CoRE

2449 Wt. W14957/M90 750,000 1/16 J.B.C. & A. Forms/C.2118/12.

Instructions regarding War Diaries and Intelligence Summaries are contained in F. S. Regs., Part II. and the Staff Manual respectively. Title Pages will be prepared in manuscript.

WAR DIARY
or
~~INTELLIGENCE SUMMARY~~
(Erase heading not required.)

Army Form C. 2118.

56 7th Coy RE

Vol 34

Place	Date	Hour	Summary of Events and Information	Remarks and references to Appendices
ACHIET-LE-PETIT	1/7/17		Inspection of arms & billets	
— " —	2/7/17		Company marched from ACHIET-LE-PETIT to LEBUCQUIERE	
LEBUCQUIERE	3/7/17		Check parade. Improving billets.	
— " —	4/7/17		3 sections Wiring at night 1 section improving coy billets	
— " —	5/7/17		— " — — " — — " —	
— " —	6/7/17		— " — — " — — " —	
— " —	7/7/17		— " — — " — — " — 1 NCO + 3 sappers Road repairs HERMIES ROAD.	
— " —	8/7/17		3 section Wiring at night 1 section improving billets 1 NCO + 6 sappers work at 9th Bde H.Q. Dugout 1 — " — 3 — " — Road repairs HERMIES ROAD	
— " —	9/7/17		2 — " — — " — — " — 1 — " — — " — 1 — " — improving billets. 1 section work on Dugout. 1 NCO + 3 sappers work on HERMIES ROAD	
— " —	10/7/17		1 section continuous reliefs on Batt H.Q. Dugout 1 section work on R.E. Dump preparing materials 1 section Night work on Dugout. 1 section Wiring. 1 NCO + 3 sappers work on HERMIES ROAD	
— " —	11/7/17		1 section VELU WOOD + in camp preparing timber for Dugouts, camouflage etc 1 — " — Continuous reliefs on Batt H.Q. Dugout 2 sections Wiring. 1 NCO + 4 HERMIES ROAD 1 — " — — " — — " — 1 section Taping out New C.T. + work on Dugouts	
— " —	12/7/17		1 — " — Work on R.E. Dump. + in camp preparing materials. 1 NCO + 4 sappers work on HERMIES ROAD 1 — " — Night work on Dugouts etc	

2449 Wt. W14957/M90 750,000 1/16 J.B.C. & A. Forms/C.2118/12.

Army Form C. 2118.

Instructions regarding War Diaries and Intelligence Summaries are contained in F. S. Regs., Part II. and the Staff Manual respectively. Title Pages will be prepared in manuscript.

WAR DIARY
or
INTELLIGENCE SUMMARY
(Erase heading not required.)

Place	Date	Hour	Summary of Events and Information	Remarks and references to Appendices
LE BOCQUIERE	13/7/17	—	3 Officers 2 sections + 360 Infantry digging C.T. 1 section continuous relief on Batt HQ Dugout 1 section work in Camp & RE Dump preparing material. 1 NCO + 4 sappers [illegible] HERMIES Road.	
— " —	14/7/17	—	3 Officers + 2 sections work on C.T. 1 section continuous work on Batt HQ Dugout 1 section work in camp & at RE Dump preparing materials. 1 Officer & 5 OR laying brick on track to HERMIES	
— " —	15/7/17		2 Officers and 1 sections + 360 Infantry digging C.T. 1 Officer + section continuous relief on Batt HQ Dugouts; 1 section preparing materials, in camp. 1 Officer + section constructing Dugout for Bde HQ. 1 Officer + 5 OR repairing track to HERMIES. 4 sappers supervising Infantry on Dugouts.	
— " —	16/7/17		2 Officers + 1 section, 228 Infantry work on C.T. 1 Officer + section continuous relief on Batt HQ Dugout 1 Officer — " — Constructing Bde HQ Dugout. 1 section preparing materials etc.	
— " —	17/7/17		1 Officer + section work on C.T. 2 sections work on Dugouts 1 section preparing material & improving billets 1 NCO + 3 sappers Road repair.	
— " —	18/7/17		— " — — " —	
— " —	19/7/17		— " — — " —	
— " —	20/7/17		1 Officer + section work on C.T. + Dugout. 2 sections work on Dugouts. 1 section work in camp & RE Dump preparing material and improving billets 1 NCO + 3 sappers Road repair.	
	21/7/17		— " —	

2449 Wt. W14957/M90 750,000 1/16 J.B.C. & A. Forms/C.2118/12.

Army Form C. 2118.

Instructions regarding War Diaries and Intelligence Summaries are contained in F. S. Regs., Part II. and the Staff Manual respectively. Title Pages will be prepared in manuscript.

WAR DIARY
or
INTELLIGENCE SUMMARY

(Erase heading not required.)

Place	Date	Hour	Summary of Events and Information	Remarks and references to Appendices
LEBUCQUIERE	22/7/17		1 Officer & section work on C.T. & Dugout. 2 Officers & 2 sections work on deep Dugouts. 1 section work in camp and at R.E. Dump preparing materials & improving Billets 1 NCO & 2 sappers Road repairs	
— " —	23/7/17		— " — " — " — " —	
— " —	24/7/17		— " — " — " — " —	
— " —	25/7/17		— " — " — " — " —	
— " —	26/7/17		— " — " — " — 1 NCO & 4 sappers work on [illegible] billet	
— " —	27/7/17		— " — " — " — " —	
— " —	28/7/17		— " — " — " — " —	
— " —	29/7/17		— " — " — " — 1 NCO & 2 sappers Road repairs	
— " —	30/7/17		— " — " — " — " —	
— " —	31/7/17		— " — " — " — " —	
			No 66153 Sapper Brewer B. killed in action 6/7/17	
			" 154701 — " — Thomas J. Wounded at duty — " —	
			" 140024 — " — Forsyth W.D. — " — 17-7-17	
			" 159720 — " — Dewar A. — " — 23-7-17	
			" 46292 a/2 Cpl Bowyer A. Wounded at duty 23/7/17	

[signature] Major R.E.
O.C. 56th Field Coy R.E.

2449 Wt. W14957/M90 750,000 1/16 J.B.C. & A. Forms/C.2118/12.

Instructions regarding War Diaries and Intelligence Summaries are contained in F. S. Regs., Part II. and the Staff Manual respectively. Title Pages will be prepared in manuscript.

WAR DIARY
or
~~INTELLIGENCE~~ SUMMARY
(Erase heading not required.)

Army Form C. 2118.

Original
56 Fd Coy
Vol 35

Place	Date	Hour	Summary of Events and Information	Remarks and references to Appendices
LEBUCQUIERE	1/8/17 to 4/8/17		3 Sections constructing deep Dugouts for Brigade & Battn HQrs (6 hour reliefs) 1 Section Improvements to Billets & Horse lines.	
	5/8/17 to 7/8/17		4 Sections employed in camp & Coy Horse lines.	
	8/8/17 to 20/8/17		3 Sections wiring front & intermediate lines. 1 section employed in camp & Coy Horse lines	
	21/8/17 to 28/8/17		1 Section wiring intermediate line. 2 sections constructing deep Dugouts (6 hour reliefs) 1 Section employed in camp & Coy Horse lines.	
	29/8/17 to 31/8/17		2 Sections constructing deep Dug outs & shelters. 1 Section preparing materials for T.M. Emplacement. Fixing trip rests etc. 1 section employed in camp & Coy Horse lines. (No 89329 Sapper Gage B. wounded at duty 8/8/17.)	

[illegible] Major R.E.
O.C. 56th Fd Coy R.E.
31/8/17

2449 Wt. W14957/M90 750,000 1/16 J.B.C. & A. Forms/C.2118/12.

Army Form C. 2118.

WAR DIARY
or
INTELLIGENCE SUMMARY
(Erase heading not required.)

Instructions regarding War Diaries and Intelligence Summaries are contained in F. S. Regs., Part II. and the Staff Manual respectively. Title Pages will be prepared in manuscript.

Brig 5 6 Fd Coy RE
Vol 36

Place	Date	Hour	Summary of Events and Information	Remarks and references to Appendices
LEBUCQUIERE	1/9/17		1 Section wiring intermediate line	
			1 " Constructing Dug-outs	
	2		1 " " T.M. Emplacement	
	3/9/17		1 " Work in billets	
	4/9/17		Company marched to BEHAGNIES	
BEHAGNIES	5/9/17			
"	6		Training	
	7/9/17			
"	8		Constructing Rifle range near LE TRANSLOY	
	11/9/17			
"	16		Training	
	17/9/17			
"	18/9/17		Company marched to MIRAUMONT and entrained for HOPOUTRE	
HOPOUTRE	19/9/17		" " " to VLAMERTINGHE	
VLAMERTINGHE	20/9/17			
			All sections erecting NISSEN HUTS	
	25			
	28/9/17			
	29/9/17		Dismounted portion marched to YPRES	
YPRES	30/9/17		All sections constructing MULE TRACKS & ROADS	
	24/9/17			
	30/9/17		Dismounted portion marched to BRANDHOEK	

Casualties

41742 Sapper Hawthorne A. wounded 25/9/17
23965 Pioneer Durrant F.
80037 " Dean S.
33342 " Pritchard S.
58835 " Walsh R.

(the last four bracketed: wounded 28/9/17)

A. W. Urwin. Major RE.
OC 56th Fd Coy RE.

2449 Wt. W14957/M90 750,000 1/16 J.B.C. & A. Forms/C.2118/12.

Army Form C. 2118.

Instructions regarding War Diaries and Intelligence Summaries are contained in F. S. Regs., Part II. and the Staff Manual respectively. Title Pages will be prepared in manuscript.

WAR DIARY
or
INTELLIGENCE SUMMARY
(Erase heading not required.)

56 Fd Coy R.E.
Original
Vol 37

Place	Date	Hour	Summary of Events and Information	Remarks and references to Appendices
BRANDHOEK	1/10/17		Dismounted embussed for WINNEZEELE. Mounted portion proceeded by march route.	
WINNEZEELE	2/10/17		Resting.	
— " —	3/10/17		Mounted section proceeded by march route to WISERNES	
	4/10/17		Dismounted embussed for WISERNES	
WISERNES	5/10/17		whole Company entrained for BAPAUME & marched from BAPAUME to YTRES	
YTRES	6/10/17		Resting.	
	7/10 8/10		3 sections constructing stables. 2 sections training	
FAVREUIL	9/10/17		Company marched to FAVREUIL. 3 sections proceeded to forward billets at NOREUIL.	
NOREUIL	10/10/17 14/10/17		3 Sections on framing Trench boarding & revetting C.T.s & support line	
"	15/10/17 21/10/17		2½ Sections — Do — 6 sappers working on M.G. nests	
"	22/10/17 to 31/10/17		2 Sections less 6 sappers on framing revetting C.T.s & support line. 6 sappers working on M.G. nests. 1 Section night work. Wiring front & support lines.	
			Sections worked in reliefs of 12 days in forward area & 4 days at Rear billet. The section in Rear billet was employed in constructing a hutted camp.	

[signature]
31/10/17
Major R.E.
O.C. 56th Field Coy R.E.

2449 Wt. W14957/M90 750,000 1/16 J.B.C. & A. Forms/C.2118/12.

Army Form C. 2118.

Original

WAR DIARY
~~or~~
~~INTELLIGENCE SUMMARY~~
(Erase heading not required.)

56 Fd Coy R.E.

56th Field Coy RE

Vol 38

Instructions regarding War Diaries and Intelligence Summaries are contained in F. S. Regs., Part II. and the Staff Manual respectively. Title Pages will be prepared in manuscript.

Place	Date	Hour	Summary of Events and Information	Remarks and references to Appendices
NOREUIL	1/4/17 to 6/4/17	–	2 Sections framing & revetting C.T.s and Support Line. 6 sappers working on Machine Gun dug-outs. 1 Section working by night on Wiring Front line and Support line. 1 Section erecting huts at MORY.	
	4/4/17		Capt. WHITE left the Coy to be adjt R.E. of 11th Div R.E.	
	6/4/17	–	3 Sections returned to rear billets at FAVREUIL.	
	6/4/17 to 19/4/17		worked on Gum Boot store at FAVREUIL.	
	7/4/17		1 Section hutting at MORY.	
	8/4/17 to 14/4/17		4 Sections do.	
	15/4/17		2 Sections do.	
	16/4/17 to 18/4/17		2 Sections worked on Drainage Trenches.	
	18/4/17 to 19/4/17		2 " erected " " behind front line.	
	20/4/17 to 25/4/17	–	3 Sections worked on clearing road through BULLECOURT.	
	26/4/17		4 Sections resting.	
	27/4/17		4 Sections hutting at MORY.	
	28/4/17		3 Sections resting. Remainder hutted at MORY.	
	29/4/17 to 30/4/17		4 Sections hutting at MORY.	

[signature] Major R.E.
O.C. 56th Field Coy R.E.

2449 Wt. W14957/M90 750,000 1/16 J.B.C. & A. Forms/C.2118/12.

Instructions regarding War Diaries and Intelligence Summaries are contained in F. S. Regs., Part II. and the Staff Manual respectively. Title Pages will be prepared in manuscript.

Army Form C. 2118.

WAR DIARY
or
INTELLIGENCE SUMMARY
(Erase heading not required.)

VII original 39

Place	Date	Hour	Summary of Events and Information	Remarks and references to Appendices
FAVREUIL	1/12/17 to 6/12/17		4 Sections hutting at MORY	
	7/12/17		Captain F.M. DEAN proceeded to RE school of Instruction	
	7/12/17 to 9/12/17		4 Sections wiring TOWER SUPPORT Trench near BULLECOURT	
	10/12/17		" standing by.	
	11/12/17		3 " moved to forward billets at NOREUIL	
NOREUIL	12/12/17 to 14/12/17		3 " wiring supports + constructing firebays 1 " Hutting at MORY.	
	15/12/17		Transport moved from Rear billets at FAVREUIL to rear billets at MORY. 3 Sections digging new trench between WINDY CORNER + HORSE SHOE REDOUBT	
	16/12/17 to 19/12/17		3 sections wiring in Front of + deepening TOWER Trench	
	19/12/17		Temp. 2/Lieut. T.C. FAGG joined from RE Base Depot	
	20/12/17		3 sections improving company forward billets at NOREUIL	
	21/12/17		" digging new trench between LONDON SUPPORT + TOWER SUPPORT	
	22/12/17		" moved from forward billets at NOREUIL to rear billets at MORY	
	16/12/17 to 22/12/17		1 " constructing Camp at MORY	
MORY	23/12/17 to 24/12/17		4 sections supervising work of Infy of 9th Infy Bde on wiring, digging + Erecting Elephant Shelters on RAILWAY RESERVE + TANK AVENUE	
	25/12/17		XMAS day (No work)	

2449 Wt. W14957/M90 750,000 1/16 J.B.C. & A. Forms/C.2118/12.

Instructions regarding War Diaries and Intelligence Summaries are contained in F. S. Regs., Part II. and the Staff Manual respectively. Title Pages will be prepared in manuscript.

WAR DIARY
or
INTELLIGENCE SUMMARY
(Erase heading not required.)

Army Form C. 2118.

Original

Place	Date	Hour	Summary of Events and Information	Remarks and references to Appendices
~~26/12/17~~ MORY	26/12/17 + 27/12/17		4 sections Festooning + preparing for demolitions in Front + Support Lines	
	28/12/17		2 sections demolishing trenches in Front + Support Lines + two sections working in camp at MORY	
	29/12/17		4 sections festooning + demolishing trenches in Front + Support Lines	
	30/12/17		Company resting MAJOR GORDON proceeded to RE school of Instruction	
	31/12/17		4 sections at work in camp.	
			Casualties 33013 Spr. Sheppard L wounded + remains at duty 7/12/17 17277 " Drury H. " " 12/12/17 19263 " Warren A. wounded 15/12/17 43526 a/Sergt. Wallis E. " 16/12/17 108759 Sapper Midgeley A. " 18/12/17	

G.H. Day
Lt RE
for O.C.
56th Fd Co RE.

2449 Wt. W14957/M90 750,000 1/16 J.B.C. & A. Forms/C.2118/12.

3rd Division

– War Diaries

56th Field Coy R.E.

~~January, to 31st December 1918~~

1918 JAN – 1919 MAY

Instructions regarding War Diaries and Intelligence Summaries are contained in F. S. Regs., Part II. and the Staff Manual respectively. Title Pages will be prepared in manuscript.

WAR DIARY

or

~~INTELLIGENCE SUMMARY~~

(Erase heading not required.)

Army Form C. 2118.

Original

January 1918.

Vol 40

Place	Date	Hour	Summary of Events and Information	Remarks and references to Appendices
MORY	1/1/18 to 9/1/18		2 Sections Constructing Camp at MORY — " — Training	
	1/1/18		Capt F M DEAN. RE returned from RE School of Instruction	
	10/1/18		3 Sections moved to Forward billets at HENIN-SUR-COJEUIL	
HENIN	11/1/18 to 24/1/18		3 Sections Working on New Battle System + 1 Section constructing Camp at MORY.	
	18/1/18		II Lieut E. H LOAM.RE proceeded to Heavy bridging School	
	19/1/18		Major A.W. GORDON. M.C RE returned from RE School of Instruction	
	28/1/18		Mounted Section, HQ + 1 Section moved from rear billets at MORY to rear billets at BOIRY - BECQUERELLE 3 Sections moved from forward billets at HENIN CAMP to forward billets in HINDENBURG support Line.	
BOIRY.	29/1/18 to 31/1/18		3 Sections working on Trench maintenance 1 Section " at rear billet	
	30/1/18		II Lieut E. H. LOAM. RE returned from Heavy bridging School	
			Casualties	
			No 154,809 Sapper Jefferson. C.E. wounded 24/1/18	

A W Gordon Major RE
OC 56th Field Co RE

2449 Wt. W14957/M90 750,000 1/16 J.B.C. & A. Forms/C.2118/12.

56 Fd Coy RE

Vol 41

Army Form C. 2118.

WAR DIARY
or
INTELLIGENCE SUMMARY.
(Erase heading not required.)

Instructions regarding War Diaries and Intelligence Summaries are contained in F. S. Regs., Part II. and the Staff Manual respectively. Title pages will be prepared in manuscript.

Place	Date	Hour	Summary of Events and Information	Remarks and references to Appendices
BOIRY BECQUERELLE	1/2/18 to 11/2/18		3 Sections worked on trench maintenance. No 22721 2/Cpl PREECE. F. attended RE Bridging school & obtained "skilled" for general qualifications for bridging. (course from 1/2/18 to 13/2/18).	
	12/2/18 to 28/2/18		2 Sections do.	
			1 " constructing new Brigade H.Q.	
			1 " Erecting huts, constructing baths & working in rear billets	
			On 20/2/18 No 6450 A/Farrier Sergt MILLS A.R. was relieved by No. 546443 Farrier Sergt HOBBS. F. and was sent to RE. Base Depot for transfer to U. K.	
			Casualties 1/2/18 – 28/2/18	
	10/2/18		No 145609 Sapper SHAW. J. wounded	

A W Linton Major RE.
O.C. 56th Field Coy RE.

3rd Divisional Engineers

56th FIELD COMPANY R. E.

MARCH 1918

CRE 3rd Division F.101 3rd

Enclosed please find War Diary of this Unit for the Month of March 1918

1/4/18

[signature] Major RE
OC 56th Field Co RE

Army Form C. 2118.

Vol. 42

Instructions regarding War Diaries and Intelligence Summaries are contained in F. S. Regs., Part II. and the Staff Manual respectively. Title pages will be prepared in manuscript.

WAR DIARY
or
~~INTELLIGENCE~~ SUMMARY.

(Erase heading not required.)

56th Field Co RE

Place	Date	Hour	Summary of Events and Information	Remarks and references to Appendices
BOIRY BECQUERELLE	1/3/18 to 20/3/18		3 Sections working on Trench Maintenance & new Brigade HQ + constructing Minefield 1 Section working at rear Billets on baths etc (Sections worked in reliefs of 12 days, 2 sections at Forward billets & 2 Sections at rear Billets)	
	21/3/18		HQ, 2 Sections & Transport moved by march route to WAILLY	
WAILLY	22/3/18		2 Sections moved by march route from forward billets to WAILLY 2 Sections worked on new battle System	
	23/3/18		4 Sections resting	
	24/3/18 to 28/3/18		4 Sections worked on New Battle system	
	28/3/18		4 Sections manned Trenches until relieved at 4 am on 29/3/18 HQ & Transport moved to GROSVILLE by march route 4 Sections returned to H.Q. at GROSVILLE	
GROSVILLE	29/3/18		Company moved by march route to MONCHIET + afterwards to GOUY-en-Artois	
GOUY-en-Artois	30/3/18		" " " " " IVERGNY	
IVERGNY	31/3/18		" Resting	

Casualties

No 26779 Sapper Hemmings. H. Wounded in action 25/3/18
" 11525 " Rathband. F. " " 26/3/18
" 140433 2/Cpl Vanstone. C. C Killed " " 28/3/18
" 33058 Sapper Gordery. A. Wounded " " 28/3/18

A W Gordon Major RE
OC 56th Field Co RE

(A7092). Wt. W12839/M1293. 750,000. 1/17. D. D. & L., Ltd. Forms/C.2118/14

3rd Divisional Engineers

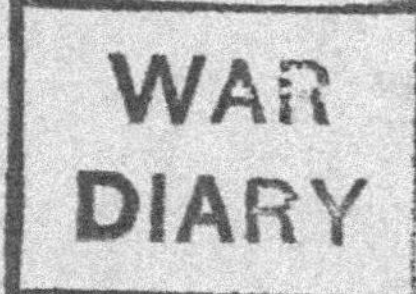

56th FIELD COMPSNY R. E.

APRIL 1 9 1 8

Instructions regarding War Diaries and Intelligence Summaries are contained in F. S. Regs., Part II. and the Staff Manual respectively. Title pages will be prepared in manuscript.

WAR DIARY
or
~~INTELLIGENCE SUMMARY.~~

(Erase heading not required.)

Army Form C. 2118.

56th Field Coy RE

Place	Date	Hour	Summary of Events and Information	Remarks and references to Appendices
IVERGNY	1 4/18		Company moved to BEUGIN, Dismounted by bus + Transport by march route.	Vol 43
BEUGIN	2 4/18 to 4 4/18		Training	
	4 4/18		Company moved by March route to OURTON.	
OURTON	5 4/18 + 6 4/18		Training	
	7 4/18		Company moved by march route to HERSIN.	
HERSIN	8 4/18 to 11 4/18		Working on Army Line (digging trenches + wiring)	
	11 4/18		Company moved to OBLINGHEM, dismounted personel by bus + Transport by march route	
OBLINGHEM	12 4/18 + 13 4/18		Digging trenches + wiring	
	14 4/18		Company moved by march route to ANNEZIN.	
ANNEZIN	14 4/18 to 30 4/18		Digging trenches, wiring, bridging, preparing bridges for demolition + standing by to demolish same + Constructing Battalion Headquarters.	

<u>Casualties</u>

No 18145 a/CSM. Ferguson H. "wounded + remained at duty" 18 4/18
21437 a/c P L/Cpl Howell. A "wounded" 21 4/18
430388 Sapper Prescott. W.A. " " 24 4/18
209173 Driver Brookes. H " 26 4/18
21094 " Robbins. H. " + remained at duty 26 4/18
22141 Sapper Hammond J. "wounded" 29 4/18 (died of wounds same day)

A W Cowan Major RE
OC 56th Field Coy RE

(A7092). Wt. W12839/M1293. 750,000. 1/17. D. D. & L., Ltd. Forms/C.2118/14.

Instructions regarding War Diaries and Intelligence Summaries are contained in F. S. Regs., Part II. and the Staff Manual respectively. Title pages will be prepared in manuscript.

WAR DIARY
or
~~INTELLIGENCE SUMMARY.~~
(Erase heading not required.)

Army Form C. 2118.

56th Field Coy RE

VR 44

Place	Date	Hour	Summary of Events and Information	Remarks and references to Appendices
Annezin	1 5/18		Company Resting. Inspection of Arms etc.	
	2 5/18 to 3 5/18		Working on Concrete Machine Gun Emplacements	
	11 5/18 to 12 5/18		Bridging & preparing bridges for demolition & Guarding bridges for demolition & constructing Batt. HQ	
	12 5/18		Section moved to rear billet at sheet 36 B. D.24.a central	
D.24.a central	13 5/18		3 Sections resting, 1 Section measuring & reconnoitring bridges & working on Div: baths	
	14 5/18 to 16 5/18		3 Sections preparing bridges for demolition & 1 Section working on divisional baths	
	16 5/18		4 Sections moved to forward billets at ANNEZIN.	
ANNEZIN	16 5/18 to 30 5/18		Bridging, Guarding bridges for demolition, Constructing Brigade HQ, R.F.A HQ. Regimental Aid Post & Machine Gun Emplacements	
	30 5/18		2 Sections & HQ moved to rear billet at sheet 36 B. D.24.a central	
D.24.a central	31 5/18		2 Sections resting & 2 Sections working on Machine Gun Emplacements	

Casualties

No 26553 a/Sergt Edwards F
" 22721 a/Corpl Preece F
" 22704 a/L/Cl Buckley G
" 140419 a/2 Cpl Dickson G
552725 Sapper Ashton PW
2322?? " Alexander D
2?8094 " Brooking FW
19803 " Battersby J
140408 " Baker E

No 94251 Sapper Cooke A
41793 " Clarke WH
518766 " Cousins A
133416 " Horne A
223906 " Knowles GF
33825 " Long LT
139890 " Mallet WG
437768 " Mulus W
2444368 " Rolfe G
96362 Dvr Rogers CH
459076 Spr Robson HR

No 420301 Sapper Reid D
540867 " Smith SJ
202311 " Spratt HE
157301 " Starling V
159438 " Shaw E
23712 " Sangrouber? W
120729 " Hatson W
554350 " White GH

"Wounded Gas" 2/5/18

(A7092). Wt. W12839/M1293 750,000. 1/17. D. D. & L., Ltd. Forms/C.2118/14.

Army Form C. 2118.

Instructions regarding War Diaries and Intelligence Summaries are contained in F. S. Regs., Part II. and the Staff Manual respectively. Title pages will be prepared in manuscript.

WAR DIARY
or
INTELLIGENCE SUMMARY.
(Erase heading not required.)

56th Field Co RE

Place	Date	Hour	Summary of Events and Information	Remarks and references to Appendices
			Casualties continued	
			" Lieut F H Loam RE "Killed in Action" 7/5/18	
			No 487066 Sapper Holmes T A } "Wounded Gas" 22/5/18	
			" 540896 " Lower J } remained at duty	
			" 33446 " Curtis H J "Wounded" 25/5/18	
			" 160370 " Aldworth F "Wounded" 29/5/18	
			31/5/18	
			A W Corbin Major RE OC 56th Field Coy RE	

(A7092). Wt. W12839/M1293. 750,000. 1/17. D. D. & L., Ltd. Forms/C.2118/14.

Instructions regarding War Diaries and Intelligence Summaries are contained in F. S. Regs., Part II. and the Staff Manual respectively. Title pages will be prepared in manuscript.

WAR DIARY
or
~~INTELLIGENCE SUMMARY.~~
(Erase heading not required.)

Army Form C. 2118.

56th Field Coy. R.E.

45

Place	Date	Hour	Summary of Events and Information	Remarks and references to Appendices
D.24.a.central	1 6/18 to 4 6/18		2 Sections at Forward billets at ANNEZIN working on Machine Gun Emplacements 2 " at Rear billets at D.24.a.central removing charges from bridges and working in camp etc.	
— " —	4 6/18		2 Sections and Headquarters moved to forward billets ANNEZIN.	
ANNEZIN	5 6/18 to 30 6/18		Constructing concrete Machine Gun Emplacements + dugouts, Guarding bridges + barges for demolition, Fixing gas-blankets, Erecting Steel shelters for Bde. HQ. and Trench Mortar Batty. HQ., Digging, repairing, and revetting Trenches etc.	
			Casualties No. 180726 Sapper Young J. "wounded" 15 6/18 " 167101 " Lavender R. " remained at duty 15 6/18 " 89185 " Brooks A.G. " " " 17 6/18 " 103478 " Andrews W. " 18 6/18	
	30 6/18			

A. W. Gordon Major R.E.
O.C. 56th Field Co R.E.

(A7092). Wt. W12839/M1293. 750,000. 1/17. D. D. & L., Ltd. Forms/C.2118/14.

Army Form C. 2118.

WAR DIARY
or
~~INTELLIGENCE~~ SUMMARY.
(*Erase heading not required.*)

Instructions regarding War Diaries and Intelligence Summaries are contained in F. S. Regs., Part II. and the Staff Manual respectively. Title pages will be prepared in manuscript.

56th Field Coy RE

Place	Date	Hour	Summary of Events and Information	Remarks and references to Appendices
ANNEZIN	1/7/18 to 31/7/18		4 Sections worked on Concrete M.G. Emplacements + dugouts, Trench Maintenance, and Guarding bridges + barges for demolition.	VII 46
			Transfers	
			No. 14721, a/Sergt Woods B.E. to R.E. Base Depot. for transfer to U.K. 5/7/18	
			7593, C.Q.M.S. Walshaw J.T. " " " 26/7/18	
			Casualties	
			No. 213539 Sapper Berry W. "Wounded 22/7/18"	
	1/8/18		A.M. Gordon Major RE. O.C. 56th Field Coy RE.	WC

(A7092). Wt. W12839/M1293. 750,000. 1/17. D. D. & L., Ltd. Forms/C.2118/14.

Army Form C. 2118.

V82 47

Instructions regarding War Diaries and Intelligence Summaries are contained in F. S. Regs., Part II. and the Staff Manual respectively. Title pages will be prepared in manuscript.

WAR DIARY
or
~~INTELLIGENCE SUMMARY.~~

(Erase heading not required.)

56th Field Co RE — August 1918.

Place	Date	Hour	Summary of Events and Information	Remarks and references to Appendices
Annezin	1/8 to 6/8/18		Work on Trench Maintenance, erecting concrete dugouts, Machine Gun emplacements etc + guarding bridges for demolitions etc	
	7/8/18		Company moved by march route to RAIMBERT.	
RAIMBERT	7/8 to 13/8/18		Training	
	13/8/18		Dismounted personnel moved by train + mounted Personnel by march route to BREVILLERS	
BREVILLERS	14/8 to 19/8/18		Training	
	19/8/18		4 Sections moved to HANNESCAMPS + remainder of Company to BIENVILLERS-au-BOIS.	
BIENVILLERS AU BOIS	20/8/18		1 Section moved forward to work with 9th Inf Bde 3 Section moved to forward Billets	
	21/8 to 24/8/18		Company working on roads etc	
	22/8/18		Capt F. B. Kenny RE Joined as OC from 7th Field Co RE	
	24/8/18		Company moved to Purple Line near DOUCHY les AYETTE	
	25/8 to 28/8/18		Work on roads etc	
	27/8/18		1 Section moved forward to work with 9th Inf Bde	
	28/8/18		Company moved to "The Halt" at 57c. S 10. d. 7. 4.	
57c. S10.d.7.4	28/8 to 31/8/18		Sections working on forward roads forward div HQ etc	

Casualties

Major A. N. Gordon MC } killed in Action 6/8/18
48531 Sapper Boys H
108587 " Mang G "wounded in Action" 22/8/18
34454 " Bowles A }
434666 " Harriott J H } killed in Action 23/8/18

No 183214 Spr Hepburn G. Died of Wounds 23/8/18
32990 " Bunch E }
112333 " Blazow F } Wounded in
33053 " Fowler T } Action 23/8/18
134920 " Veale C }

F. B. Kenny Major RE
OC 56th Field Co RE

(A7092). Wt. W12839/M1293. 750,000. 1/17. D. D. & L., Ltd. Forms/C.2118/14.

Instructions regarding War Diaries and Intelligence Summaries are contained in F. S. Regs., Part II. and the Staff Manual respectively. Title pages will be prepared in manuscript.

WAR DIARY
or
~~INTELLIGENCE SUMMARY.~~
(Erase heading not required.)

3rd Dvn

Army Form C. 2118.

56th Field Coy. R.E. September. 1918

Place	Date	Hour	Summary of Events and Information	Remarks and references to Appendices
57.C S10.d.7.4.	1.9/18 to 2.9/18		Working on Forward roads etc.	
	3 9/18		Moved by March route to 57.C. a.10.d.6.2.	
	4 9/18 to 5 9/18		Moved to St LEGER & worked on Forward roads etc.	
St. LEGER	6 9/18		Moved by March Route to POMMIER	
POMMIER	7 9/18 to 10 9/18		Training	
	11 9/18		Moved by March Route to ABLAINZEVILLE	
ABLAINZEVILLE	12 9/18		" " " " MORT-HOMME near St LEGER	
MORT-HOMME	13 9/18		Working on Forward roads etc	
	14 9/18		Moved by March Route to BEUGNY	
BEUGNY	16 9/18		" " " " 57.C. J.26.b.7.6	
J.26.b.7.6	16 9/18 to 29 9/18		Working on forward roads etc. & Bridged Canal du Nord on 26/9/18 at Sheet 57.C K.20.b.4.6 between BELL TRENCH & JERMYN STREET	
	30 9/18		Moved by March Route to HAVRINCOURT	

V 8 48

(A7092). Wt. W12839/M1293. 750,000. 1/17. D. D. & L., Ltd. Forms/C.2118/14.

Instructions regarding War Diaries and Intelligence Summaries are contained in F. S. Regs., Part II. and the Staff Manual respectively. Title pages will be prepared in manuscript.

WAR DIARY
or
INTELLIGENCE SUMMARY.
(Erase heading not required.)

Army Form C. 2118.

Place	Date	Hour	Summary of Events and Information	Remarks and references to Appendices
			Casualties	
			Lieut J.W. Ings.	
			166479 Spr. Billsborough S — Killed in Action 18/9/18	
			470866 " Patterson J	
			486533 " Sadler J.	
			24242 a/Sergt. Kellie J.H.	
			103056 L/Cpl McCrone D.J.	
			14239 Sapper Bell R.	
			160093 " Bower T — Wounded in Action 18/9/18	
			50334 " Dodds J.H.	
			167101 " Savender R	
			170480 " Ramsay J	
			F.B.K[illegible] Major R.E.	
			O.C. 56th Field Co R.E.	
			1/10/18	

(A7092). Wt. W12839/M1293. 750,000. 1/17. D. D. & L., Ltd. Forms/C.2118/14.

13

Army Form C. 2118.

WAR DIARY
or
~~INTELLIGENCE SUMMARY.~~
(Erase heading not required.)

Instructions regarding War Diaries and Intelligence Summaries are contained in F. S. Regs., Part II. and the Staff Manual respectively. Title pages will be prepared in manuscript.

56th Field Coy RE

Vol 49

Place	Date	Hour	Summary of Events and Information	Remarks and references to Appendices
HAVRINCOURT	1/10/18		Company moved by march Route to FLESQUIERES	
FLESQUIERES	9/10/18		" " " " " to HAVRINCOURT	
HAVRINCOURT	13/10/18		" " " " " to MARCOING	
MARCOING	20/10/18		" " " " " " BEVILLERS	
BEVILLERS	22/10/18		" " " " " " QUIEVY.	
QUIEVY	23/10/18		" " " " " " SOLESMES	
SOLESMES	24/10/18		" " " " " " ROMERIES	
ROMERIES	27/10/18		" " " " " " ESCARMAIN	
ESCARMAIN	30/10/18		" " " " " " SOLESMES.	
SOLESMES	31/10/18		" " " " " " CATTENIERES	
	1/10/18 to 31/10/18		The Company has been employed on Bridging, Repairing Bridges + Roads water supply etc.	
			Casualties Nil.	
	31/10/18		E. [signature] Major RE OC 56th Field Coy RE	

(A7092). Wt. W12839/M1293. 750,000. 1/17. D. D. & L., Ltd. Forms/C.2118/14.

Instructions regarding War Diaries and Intelligence Summaries are contained in F. S. Regs., Part II. and the Staff Manual respectively. Title pages will be prepared in manuscript.

WAR DIARY
or
~~INTELLIGENCE SUMMARY.~~
(Erase heading not required.)

Army Form C. 2118.

56th Field Co RE

Place	Date	Hour	Summary of Events and Information	Remarks and references to Appendices
CATTENIERES	1/11/18 to 3/11/18		Coy Resting	VR 50
	3/11/18		Company moved by March Route to SOLESMES	
SOLESMES	4/11/18		" " " " " ESCARMAIN	
ESCARMAIN	5/11/18		" " " " " ORSINVAL	
ORSINVAL	6/11/18 to 16/11/18		" Resting & Training	
	16/11/18		" Moved by March Route to LA LONGUEVILLE	
LA LONGUEVILLE	18/11/18		" " " " " SOUS-LE-BOIS	
SOUS-LE-BOIS	20/11/18		" " " " " OSTERGNIES	
	21/11/18 to 23/11/18		" Resting & Training	
	24/11/18		" Moved by March Route to BIERCEE	
BIERCEE	25/11/18		" " " " " BERZEE	
BERZEE	26/11/18		" " " " " VILLERS POTERIE	
	28/11/18		" " " " " St GERARD	
St GERARD	29/11/18		" " " " " DURINNE	
DURINNE	30/11/18		" " " " " DURNAL	

From 3/11/18 to 6/11/18 Company was employed on repairs to Forward Roads & Bridges

E B [signature] Major RE
OC 56th Field Co RE

(A7092). Wt. W12839/M1293. 750,000. 1/17. D. D. & L., Ltd. Forms/C.2118/14.

Instructions regarding War Diaries and Intelligence Summaries are contained in F. S. Regs., Part II. and the Staff Manual respectively. Title pages will be prepared in manuscript.

WAR DIARY
or
~~INTELLIGENCE SUMMARY.~~
(Erase heading not required.)

Army Form C. 2118.

56th Field Co RE

Place	Date	Hour	Summary of Events and Information	Remarks and references to Appendices
DORINNE	1/12/18		Company moved by march route to DURNAL	
DURNAL	1/12/18 to 4/12/18		Resting & cleaning equipment etc	
"	4/12/18		Company moved by march route to SCY.	
SCY	5/12/18		" " " " " to MONTEUVILLE	
MONTEUVILLE	6/12/18		" " " " " " FISENNE	
FISENNE	7/12/18		" " " " " " OSTER-le-BALLY.	
OSTER-LE-BALLY	8/12/18		" " " " " " FRAITURE	
FRAITURE	9/12/18		" " " " " " HEBRONVAL	
HEBRONVAL	10/12/18		Resting	
	11/12/18		Company " " " " " DEYFELDT.	
DEYFELDT	12/12/18		Crossed border into Germany " " NEUNDORF	
NEUNDORF	13/12/18		" " " " " " ANDLER	
ANDLER	14/12/18		" " " " " " FRAUENKRON	
FRAUENKRON	15/12/18		" " " " " " BLANKENHEIM	
BLANKENHEIM	16/12/18		" " " " " " HOLZMULHEIM	
HOLZMULHEIM	17/12/18		" " " " " " EVERSHEIM	
EVERSHEIM	18/12/18		" " " " " " KESSINICH.	
KESSINICH	19/12/18		" " " " " " FROITZHEIM.	
FROITZHEIM	20/12/18		" " " " " " DUREN.	
DUREN	21/12/18 to 31/12/18		Improving billets, constructing cookhouses, ablution benches, latrines, etc	

31/12/18

[illegible] Major RE
OC 56th Field Coy RE

(A7092). Wt. W12839/M1293. 750,000. 1/17. D. D. & L., Ltd. Forms/C.2118/14.

Instructions regarding War Diaries and Intelligence Summaries are contained in F. S. Regs., Part II. and the Staff Manual respectively. Title pages will be prepared in manuscript.

WAR DIARY
or
~~INTELLIGENCE SUMMARY.~~
(Erase heading not required.)

Army Form C. 2118.

56th Field Co RE

Place	Date	Hour	Summary of Events and Information	Remarks and references to Appendices
DUREN	1/1/19 to 31/1/19		Improving Billets, Constructing cookhouses, ablution Benches, Latrines, etc + attending classes, lectures + courses in various subjects	VOL 52
	16/1/19		Major F. B. Kenny RE left unit for dispersal.	
	31/1/19		[signature] Capt RE OC 56th Field Co RE	

(A7092). Wt. W12859/M1293. 750,000. 1/17. D. D. & L., Ltd. Forms/C.2118/14.

CRE 3rd Division

attached please find War Diary of this unit for the Month of Feb 1919.

C M Young Capt RE
OC 56th Field Co RE

28/2/19

Instructions regarding War Diaries and Intelligence Summaries are contained in F. S. Regs., Part II. and the Staff Manual respectively. Title pages will be prepared in manuscript.

WAR DIARY
or
INTELLIGENCE SUMMARY.
(Erase heading not required.)

Army Form C. 2118.

VR 53

56th Field Co RE

Place	Date	Hour	Summary of Events and Information	Remarks and references to Appendices
DÜREN	1/2/19 to 24/2/19		Company employed on Improving billets, constructing Cookhouses, ablution Benches, Latrines etc + attending classes, courses and Lectures on various subjects	
	24/2/19		Company moved by march route to KERPEN.	
KERPEN	25/2/19		" " " " " to COLOGNE	
COLOGNE	25/2/19 to 28/2/19		Drill + improving billets.	
	28/2/19		C M Young Capt RE OC 56th Field Co RE.	

(A7092). Wt. W12839/M1293. 750,000. 1/17. D. D. & L., Ltd. Forms/C.2118/14.

Instructions regarding War Diaries and Intelligence Summaries are contained in F. S. Regs., Part II. and the Staff Manual respectively. Title pages will be prepared in manuscript.

WAR DIARY
or
INTELLIGENCE SUMMARY.
(Erase heading not required.)

Army Form C. 2118.

56th Field Coy RE

Vol 54

Place	Date	Hour	Summary of Events and Information	Remarks and references to Appendices
COLOGNE	1/3/19 to 31/3/19		Company employed on Erecting Delouser Plant, Cook houses, Gun Park, Stables & Guard house etc	
	31/3/19		[illegible] Major RE OC 56th Field Coy RE	

(A7092). Wt. W12839/M1293. 750,000. 1/17. D. D. & L., Ltd. Forms/C.2118/14.

3

Army Form C. 2118.

Instructions regarding War Diaries and Intelligence Summaries are contained in F. S. Regs., Part II. and the Staff Manual respectively. Title pages will be prepared in manuscript.

WAR DIARY or ~~INTELLIGENCE SUMMARY.~~

(Erase heading not required.)

56th Field Coy, RE.

Place	Date	Hour	Summary of Events and Information	Remarks and references to Appendices
COLOGNE	1/4/19 to 30/4/19		Company ordered to Reduce to Cadre "B"	
			Captain A.G. Shenstone R.E. from Hqrs C.R.E. N Division } Posted to 56th Field Company R.E. 1/4/19	
			Lieut. G.L.G. Sibley R.E.(T) " 438th Field Company R.E. }	
			" Lieut W.S. Calder R.E.(T) " 529th " " }	AGS
			" Lieut W.S. Calder R.E.(T) Demobilised, left for England 16/4/19.	
	6/4/19		Z Horses Evacuated to "White City" Cologne 3/4/19. X horses to 438, 529 & 231 Coys. Ordered to reduce to Cadre A. Y horses transferred to 438, 529 and 231 Coys on 7/4/19. Remainder of company disposed of as under.	AGS
			Parties demobilised on 9/4/19 - 8 men; 11/4/19 - 15 "; 15/4/19 - 12 "; 16/4/19 - 17 "	
			Retainable Remainder (not included in Cadre A') transferred to 438th and 529th Co R.E. 1/4/19.	AGS
			Cadre employed from 1/4/19 to 30/4/19. Checking Equipment, cleaning and painting wagons etc.	AGS

A.G. Shenstone Capt. R.E.

O.C. 56th Field Coy. R.E.

(A7092). Wt. W12839/M1293. 750,000. 1/17. D. D. & L., Ltd. Forms/C.2118/14.

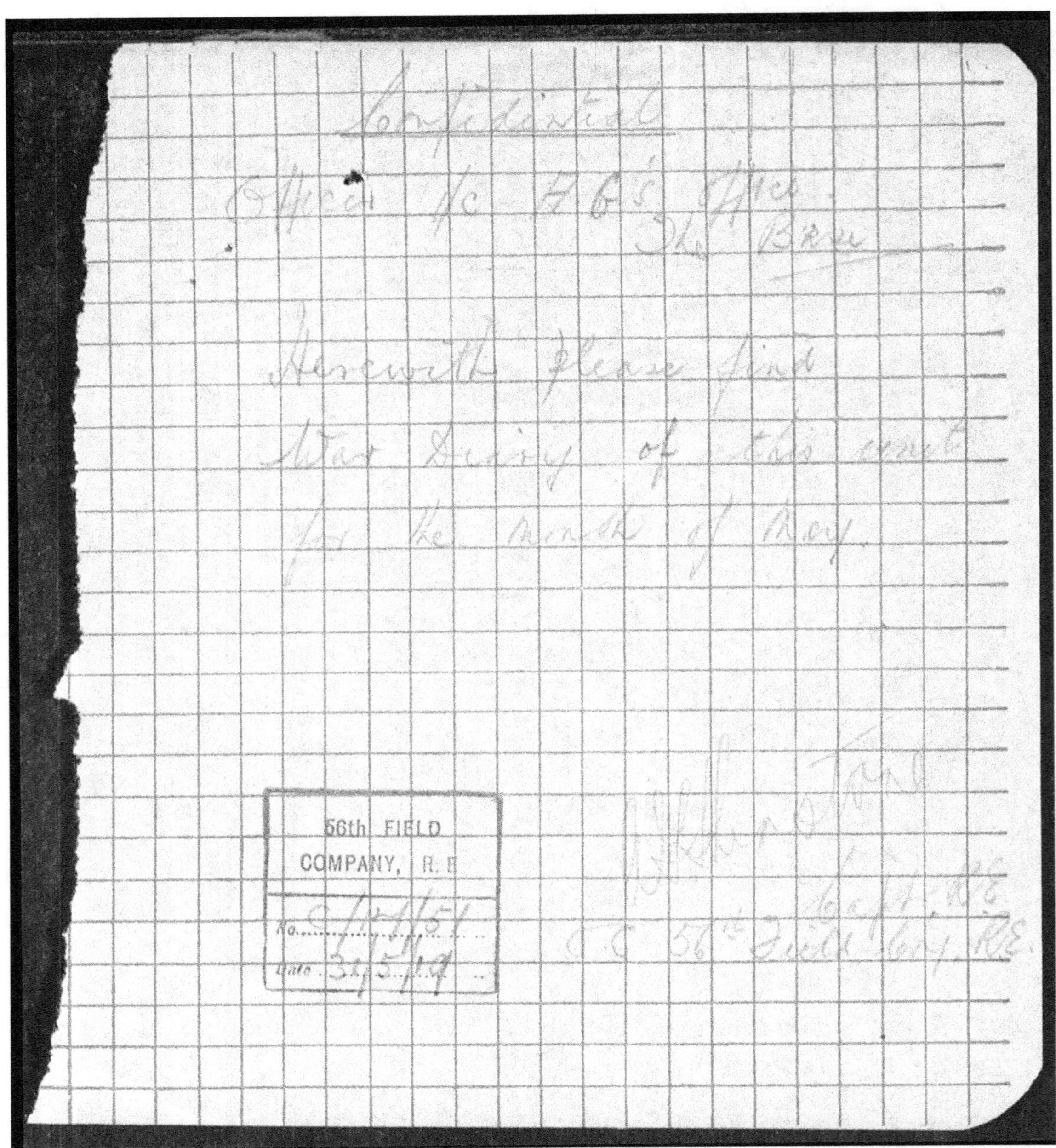

Confidential

Officer i/c A.G.'s Office
The Base

Herewith please find
War Diary of this unit
for the month of May.

56th FIELD
COMPANY, R.E.
No. C/R/51
Date 31/5/19

[illegible]
Capt. RE
O.C. 56th Field Coy. RE.

Instructions regarding War Diaries and Intelligence Summaries are contained in F. S. Regs., Part II. and the Staff Manual respectively. Title pages will be prepared in manuscript.

WAR DIARY

or

~~INTELLIGENCE~~ SUMMARY.

(*Erase heading not required.*)

Army Form C. 2118.

56th Field Company, R.E.

VOL 56

Place	Date	Hour	Summary of Events and Information	Remarks and references to Appendices
COLOGNE	1/3/19 to 4/3/19.		Checking Equipment and painting wagons.	[illegible]
	5/3/19		Company moved from LINDENTHAL to FLORA GARTEN. Change billets with 132 A T CORE [?]	[illegible]
	6/3/19 to 31/3/19		Company employed on painting and labelling wagons and making preparations for moving to BULFORD.	[illegible]

COLOGNE
31/3/19

A G Shenstone [?]
Capt RE.
OC 56th Field CORE

(A7092). Wt. W12839/M1293. 750,000. 1/17. D. D. & L., Ltd. Forms/C.2118/14.

www.ingramcontent.com/pod-product-compliance
Lightning Source LLC
Chambersburg PA
CBHW080850230426
43662CB00013B/2065